Cultivate Growth!

A guide to successful leadership

Anders Berglund

ISBN: 1505651182
ISBN   13- 9781505651188

Contents

Background   11

Culture: The Environment We Are Trying to Support

Intro to Culture   20

Trust   25

Keep on Rolling!   32

No Cost Budget   37

Generosity   41

Informal Structure   44

Fun   56

Gardeners: The Way We Lead.

Intro to Gardeners   65

Self-Awareness   72

Leading by Example   75

Confront with Love!   80

Fire with Love!   85

Team Leadership   90

Project Groups 96

I see you...! I am here! 98

Leadership & Personal Develop. 106

Personal Plans of Action 111

Plants: Reaching All Our Coworkers, Regardless of Why We "Landed Here" to Begin With.

Intro to Our Plants 117

The University of Our Store 121

Recovery 130

Internal Promotions 134

Hiring of Relatives 139

My Own Journey 142

End Result

150

Now It's Up to You!

153

Appendix: Our Training

157

Introduction

After reading this book, I asked Anders if I could write the introduction. We met in 1979 when I needed someone to help me turn around six company stores in Canada that were in deep financial trouble, Anders started as the financial "wiz," but I later noticed that he was a man of many trades. We had an immediate strong bond that has lasted to this day and I hope for the rest of our days. Yes, I was his "boss" over many years, but what is a good boss if he doesn't surround himself with the best people, leaders, and ultimately friends he can find?

Anders is a great leader and developer of people, helping them find their inner potential. He talks about the gardener, the one who can find the smallest seed in someone, nourish it, and make it grow. I have seen how Anders can take a young person, an acorn on the lowest rung of the corporate ladder, and help them grow into a big, solid oak tree, both within our organization and then on to our parent company, unafraid to take on larger opportunities.

We have both marveled over watching these young people's development, and we have felt enormous pride in knowing we have had a part in their growth.

Anders has been my guiding light in many ways since the first day we met back in 1979. As he points out in this book, one of my roles was to support our culture by seeing the lighter side of things. He can sometimes be intense and very driven. I have seen firsthand some people become angry with him after he's confronted them with love, as he writes about in this book. But after some time they would almost invariably come up and thank him for being honest with them.

Together we managed to set a very high bar on how teamwork should be done. It was guided by a very strong mutual respect. I am so happy to have been part of our success. I helped create a public image to our customers by being responsible for our marketing, and now you will read what made our store such a huge success on the inside—the heart and soul of the company.

I will end with one of Anders's favorite and most important sayings: Let's skip the "fluff" and cut straight to the pepperoni!

Bjorn Bayley

Former President, IKEA North America

A Note from the Author

This book has been in development for a long time. It's been a struggle for me to correctly describe "our" story and, at the same time, try to make it a compelling one to read. Luckily, I have had many friends who have given me the en-courage-ment to go on.

I wanted to finish this book in hopes that you, the reader, would find some of the ideas and practices useful. You are probably a leader, or want to be a leader, for a smaller organization where the rule book is not yet written. Or you may be part of a big organization in which you have endless courage to rock the boat in your area.

Most of the ideas discussed in this book are very simple—but not easy! They may look on the surface to be incredibly simple—actually too simple, since they do not have the lure of complexity, deep thought, and professionalism. Don't let this fool you! Simple is not always easy. To make changes takes commitment and tenacity. Some would call this passion.

Reaping the benefits of trust, respect, and generosity will not happen overnight. It's a process of small steps.

On the other hand most people will probably enjoy working for you in the end! When it is all said and done, being treated with respect is what many of us strive for!

Don't give up. Your "garden" will grow, and I hope that you too will enjoy the growth of your "plants" and your organization! As you will see later in the book, we have used the metaphors of a garden and a garden center to describe what we were doing in our store.

As you will see, we have used the words *leader* and *manager* in the book where we felt they were most appropriate. The word *manager* comes from the Latin *manu agere*, which translates to "lead by the hand." For us it was less leading by the hand and more setting the stage. We felt closer to the word *leader*, and leadership was something we encouraged in every department of our store whether an employee was a formal leader or not. You will see many examples of this in the book.

Two expressions need to be explained. We used the word coworker for our employees, to better describe the nature of our collaboration. Area responsibles, were hourly paid employees that had agreed to take care of a part of our store either as part of their training to become a manager or make some extra money for assuming such a responsibility or both.

There is no way I can properly give credit to everyone who was individually responsible for our tremendous business success. It was a team effort, so I can't give credit to only certain employees. My job here is to be the storyteller. Yes, in some instances I was the person with the most passion, but nothing would have happened without all the people involved. Can this culture be re-created? I would not be telling this story if I did not firmly believe so.

A special thanks to my two partners in life: first my dear wife, Janet, my support and my love, and second, my longtime friend, mentor, and partner, Bjorn. Also thanks to all the wonderful people I had the good fortune to meet on my journey!

BACKGROUND

"When the best leader's work is done, the people say, 'We did it ourselves!'"—Lao Tzu

My partner and I were standing side by side saying farewell to some of our coworkers and their partners for the last time. The husband of one of our female coworkers came up to us and gave us both big hugs while saying, "You changed our lives; I want to thank you so much!" Over the course of the evening we heard this from many of the spouses and partners of our coworkers. What was this? I thought we had been running a furniture store? Why did we hear this over and over?

This is the story about how two long-term employees (fifty years' company experience combined) got the chance to form a partnership with the world's largest furniture company to open a store in the Seattle area to see if owner-operated stores would work better than fully company-controlled ones.

Our parent company was at the time looking for different types of setups to increase internal competition and stimulate new ideas.

It is interesting to know that most company stores in the United States were not making money in 1993 and 1994, and it was therefore easier for the company to conduct such an "experiment." In October 1994 we opened the store in Renton, south of Seattle, after a record-breaking short build-up period. But why Renton?

First, the city of Renton had a very tenacious business manager who truly believed we would bring a lot of benefits to the city. With her help and that of other city employees who accommodated the renovation project, we transformed a local warehouse into a retail outlet.

Second, this was the only location with a building that gave us the setup and financial circumstances we needed. Due to the weak economic situation for its other stores in the United States, corporate had already indicated it wanted no part of building a store for us. Its only participation was as a partner.

Previously, the location was used to produce light manufacturing for Boeing, but it was scaling down at the time. It was by no means an A+ location. It had almost none of the attributes corporate normally looks for: we had no visibility from a major freeway and were not near other retailers, and our building was not custom built.

After thirteen years of operation, our store was the largest one-level store in the world (360,000 square feet) in our company, and at one time it was on the top twenty lists of the bestselling stores worldwide! With a sales budget for the first year of $25 million, the store grew to $142 million by 2007.

In 1995 we weathered a six-month long Boeing strike on our doorstep (the buildings around us were still occupied by Boeing); then came 9/11 and the dot-com crash, when Seattle was named the epicenter of the downturn. It seems we defied the odds for becoming a success.

A few major factors led to the success of our store, local marketing being one. This book deals with something that was not so visible, but certainly could be felt by our coworkers and customers alike.

It deals with our corporate culture and our commitment to constantly grow and learn in the area of leadership. Over the years we became a learning organization. The number of employees started at 125 and grew to nearly 600. We all had to become better leaders to handle this tremendous growth.

It is interesting to see how globalization seems to make it harder and harder for good companies to keep their great cultures. Companies that were successful in the past, including Toyota, Honda, Sony, IBM, and GM, are now struggling to keep their identities in their efforts to become more bottom-line driven and less people driven. It appears that the controllers—not the engineers or charismatic leaders—decide the direction of many companies. Employees feel less loyal to companies, and therefore feel less dedication and drive. All these companies appear to be alike, with personal growth left to individuals to accomplish on their own time. Hopefully, new, smaller companies in different parts of the world will again lead the way by having an increased emphasis on supporting the growth of their people.

My hope is that this book will inspire you, the readers, to try the unusual, to not simply follow what everyone else does, and to pay the utmost attention to what cultures you are fostering in your organizations. Do not be afraid of practicing leadership! What an illusion it is to think we are either born leaders or not! Being a leader is all about hard work and struggle, realizing that there is always more you can learn and improve upon, and being humble and respectful when working with others.

Using an example of what big companies do, our parent company one year decided to employ the personal development phrase "Paddle your own canoe." While it is a good idea to encourage everyone to look after themselves in the area of leadership (since it is an "inside" job), employees do need a lot of support. Some people even need to be "pushed," like when working with plants in a garden. Some plants need to be moved to come into full bloom. We really felt it was making it too easy on us, as leaders, just to say to our employees, "Paddle your own canoe."

Our view was entirely different, and to make things clearer on how we saw personal development, we needed a better description of what we were doing that extended beyond selling home furnishings. We believed it had become our primary responsibility to encourage personal and professional growth in everyone who was employed at our store. We started to label what we did the "garden center."

We also wanted to better define employee career possibilities. In a garden center, the gardener tends to the plants to make sure they get the best possible situation for growth. Without excellent growth among the plants, the garden center will go broke, just like any business. We soon realized that without growth among our coworkers, we would not be a success.

Early in my career, I had a discussion with a consultant about a great manager in the organization that I was responsible for at the time. I was having trouble getting this manager to delegate. Suddenly the consultant said: "How do you know that this is the branch that is going to grow out next?"

At first I had no clue what she was talking about, but after further discussion I realized that she had likened a leader's growth to that of a tree. Years later it was revealed that a trust issue was to blame for the manager's reluctance to delegate. If you don't trust yourself and/or others to work effectively, it is almost impossible to delegate responsibilities. This story had a monumental impact on the way I saw leadership and growth, but for a moment let's continue our comparison with a garden center and look at what we can and cannot do for a plant.

Can: Water, fertilize, respect, protect, plant in the right soil, provide the right conditions, nurture, talk to, see if it is growing, cut, discard

Cannot: Force growth, correct, motivate to grow

If you think of yourself as a plant, what made you grow? I once asked this question at a workshop. The most common answers were: "Someone believed in me!" or "I finally started to believe in myself!" or "Someone held up a mirror in front of me so I could see myself and that I really wanted to grow!" What if we all went out gardening? Can we be more of a gardener and therefore more effective while supporting the growth of others?

Our Culture

Intro to Culture

"An organization with a strong corporate culture is like a house with a good foundation."

Culture = cultura = "to cultivate, tilling of the land"

"[C]ulture is a property of a group....Whenever a group has enough common experience, a culture begins to form. One finds cultures at the level of small teams, families, and work groups. Cultures also arise at the level of departments, functional groups, and other organizational units that have a common occupational core and common experience. Cultures are found at every hierarchical level. Culture exists at the level of the whole organization if there is sufficient shared history."—The Corporate Culture Survival Guide by Edgar H. Schein

In simple terms, if you look at a workplace as a garden, the culture in that garden is the earth that the gardener and plants are working with. The whole basic setup in the greenhouse, and the norms and rules of the whole center are dependent upon the healthy make-up of the earth being used.

In our store you could say that the overall vision and mission of our parent company, including the standards and values promoted by its leaders and especially the coworkers within the organization, determined our culture.

Obviously, the longer a person is in an organization or system, the more impact he or she can have. Climate would represent the day-to-day aspects of the operation, like the amount of watering and fertilizing that goes on. Breaking a new sales record or having slumping sales could impact the climate in the store. The climate can change quickly, whereas culture is deeper and more stable. One clearly impacts the other over time in an organization.

For us it was very important to be consistent and very tenacious to preserve both of these elements.

We wanted a great culture and a great climate, too. A good trust level is very much supported by having a good culture and climate and vice versa

A great culture, as defined by our employees themselves, meant an environment in which we truly like our fellow coworkers. "We enjoy being here. We enjoy being here together. We enjoy the company and what it represents."

A good environment in a greenhouse is essential to growing healthy plants. Likewise, a good culture is vital to the personal and professional growth of employees. And this growth is crucial for the growth of our whole business. Once our coworkers experienced this culture and enjoyed living in it, it was up to everyone to keep it alive.

Like a plant that dies when it's earth is neglected and not fertilized, culture also needs nurturing by all of us. Culture can't be maintained solely by "the bosses" or human resources (HR). We all must work together to keep our positive culture going, or it will vanish.

Many companies use HR for record keeping and prescreening new staff, as well as for firings and benefits. Just as any company needs to integrate accounting and finance into its daily operations, companies also need to make the HR department a crucial part in order to be successful.

In my view the HR department, together with a company's top manager, are both very much ultimately responsible for the culture in an organization.

At one time we formed a project group to document our culture and our way of working to help to sustain this culture while our coworker numbers were growing rapidly.

Some of us spent many hours sitting at our common lunch tables asking our employees what they thought of our store and what its culture stood for. Out of that came the following:

Our Core Values (As Defined by Our Coworkers)

Courage: "Willing to take risks by being open and honest."

Family: "A company and coworkers you can depend on."

Respect: "Treating others fairly and justly with a caring and humble approach."

Initiative: "It is up to you to make it happen."

A good corporate culture is essential for the long-term success of any organization. It will be felt not only by coworkers but by suppliers, customers, and others who come in contact with the business. As a customer, you can easily notice if the employees of an organization care about you. It often stems from whether employees feel that the organization and its leadership care about them.

TRUST

"Trust is created when I believe you are competent and that you care about me."

It took me a long time to realize how important trust is to an organization. In a world of globalization, constant staff turnover, frequent changes in organizational structures, and new CEOs coming and going, there is very little to hold on to.

One of our biggest assets became the trust our coworkers had in our organization. Of course, with that trust came a huge amount of responsibility to do the right thing.

We tried our very best to be up-front with as much information as we could and to err on the side of our coworkers in all of our dealings with them.

One of the ways we tried to deal with trust was the following: For example, a coworker would come to us and voice a complaint about a colleague. Unless it was safety related, we would ask: "What did the colleague say when you told them what you are telling me?" Almost without fail he or she had not even spoken to the person in question.

Over time we heard less and less gossip (it might still have been there), but we were prepared to pay that price for making a point. Gossip is one of the worst enemies of trust.

Another moment of truth was when an unsatisfied customer would ask us to come out onto the sales floor. It happens all the time in retail stores: a customer hopes to get a better answer from a manager. But we had been preaching to all our coworkers that they were in charge and should do what they believed would make customers happy.

The first time we walked into a situation like this, it was as if the entire store stood still. Were we going to walk the walk or were we going to overrule the coworker?

We were fully aware of the importance of this, so we were really happy to tell the customer that in our store they had already spoken to the "manager," and as far as we could see, we could do no more. Many customers commented on how impressed they were by this policy.

A few times over the years we would take a coworker (often fairly new at the job) and plead with them to be more generous toward an unsatisfied customer, but we would never overrule the coworker in front of the customer.

By trusting our coworkers and giving them many more responsibilities than most corporate stores, we reinforced our climate of trust. It really worked both ways. Many times our coworkers would take part in other store buildups or meetings and come back telling us they were allowed to do so much more than their counterparts in other stores. Our coworkers became very sought after for other store openings since they were so well trained, were used to taking charge, and could do so many different tasks.

One time early in my career, I sat with all my direct reports (fourteen of them). I was very frustrated with the lack of personal growth in our organization. I asked if they thought I trusted them and if I was giving them a lot of freedom. They all said yes and that they really liked it. I then asked, "Why are you in your turn not giving the same freedom to your staff?" They answered: "They are not ready." So my next question was: "Were you ready when I gave you this freedom?" The room went silent for a while, and in the end they all agreed that they had had their challenges in the beginning but that I had stuck with them. So here comes the big question: when and who do you trust?

My view is that we have to give out trust more freely (unless your organization is dealing with life-or-death issues). Yes, some people will not respond, but many will. People, like plants, cannot be controlled, and there is no way to know for certain if they will grow.

It often happened that our coworkers would come up with an idea they wanted to implement and we would simply say, "Run with it." Expensive ideas in which more than a few people would be involved, however, were turned down.

As you will see later in this book, we created several steps that allowed our coworkers to grow and earn our trust step by step. They were small steps for us, but often huge steps for our coworkers.

Many companies find it easier to trust someone who they find outside their organization rather than inside. Our view was totally different. Would a gardener growing locally adapted plants suddenly bring a big exotic palm tree into the garden center without extreme caution? What if it came with bugs that would kill the other plants?

Did we make many mistakes appointing someone who was not "ready"? Of course we did. That was part of the learning process for us, and the damage was often very limited.

Some people appear to have what it takes to be a success but "freeze" when in a position to be successful. Just look at sports: some athletes really bloom, and others vanish.

To continue our comparisons to a garden center, we set the stage and trusted our "plants" to do their own growing. Given the chance, they sure grew!

This doesn't just work on your coworkers. You also have to earn the trust of your customers by treating them with compassion and respect. We believe we did so, and word of mouth became one of our strongest marketing tools.

Here are some of our thoughts about trust.

- Trust is the substitute for control. Trust is both the glue and the lubricant for ensuring an effective and positive organization.
- Trust is often an inside job, meaning that you have to have trust in yourself before you can trust others.
- Trust has many different levels. You might trust someone to make you coffee, but not to take care of your children.
- Trust is something earned over time.

When Good Levels of Trust Exists in an Organization:

1. Communication is effective.
2. All energy is directed toward a common focus.
3. Issues are dealt with directly between the parties involved and not with a third person.

When Low Levels of Trust Exist:

1. There is lots of gossip.
2. There are politics.
3. Energy is lost.

How to Repair Damaged Trust:

1. Deal with the situation immediately.
2. Talk directly to the other party.
3. Take responsibility for your own actions.
4. Avoid judgments, restrictions, or control of the other person.

KEEP ON ROLLING!

"Cont-roll will stop the roll!"

Having been a controller at one time in my career, I was quite cautious, but I learned that to get good results, we have to take chances. Many companies resort to establishing enormous control systems to prevent financial losses. You can see this practice especially in bigger companies where over time a great start-up has turned into a big colossus with controls at every level.

"Cont-roll indicates stopping the roll." When you stop the roll, you might get fewer mistakes, but you also get less innovation, less risk taking, and less motivated staff. As long as your business is not involved in life-saving surgeries, it is important to keep rolling.

Many of us are trying to be perfect, so when we successfully complete a big project but maybe made a small mistake along the way, we try to put in a control system for next time. The problem is that the situations are seldom identical, and the small mistake will pop up somewhere else. Or we face a different issue in the same situation. Then, if we continue to try to plug all the "holes," in the end, we will have a product that stops the rolling, i.e. the development of our business will slow.

Do not focus on the mistakes; quickly learn what you can, and keep rolling. One day our very competent and successful marketing manager made a thirty-thousand-dollar error. In the whole scope of things, this was less than 1 percent of the money she handled on a yearly basis, but of course it was still a lot of money. She was devastated to say the least, as her strive for perfection had hit a bump in the road. I thought I needed to make a point, so I went over to her desk and stretched out my hand. She looked at me, perplexed, while I said, "Thanks for helping me realize that there are now at least two people here who are not perfect!"

Encourage your coworkers to take small risks every day. That can mean stretching the company policy to satisfy a customer or finding a new way to do something. We encouraged all staff to break as many rules as possible (except for the ones spelled out in our coworker handbook) because we had noticed that good people around the store had a tendency to implement more and more rules in an effort to do a better and better job. This seemed to be one way they could measure if they did a good job.

We believe it is impossible to write rules for everything. Life and business change fast, so rules are outdated as soon as they are written. The more structure and rules there are, the less new ideas and progress are encouraged. A very structured organization has a hard time dealing with the chaos that happens now and then to all of us.

Staff changes, bad sales, and customer complaints are just some of the things that can cause chaos in a department or even a whole store.

It is therefore extremely important that we as managers question all self-imposed rules from time to time, and ask ourselves if we really need them, so we can embrace chaos as our friend and not as our enemy.

Of course, we do not intentionally create chaos. But when it happens despite our planning, we find the lesson that can be learned in the chaotic moment. It is how we deal with chaos that defines us as managers. It's easy to be a manager in a world where nothing unexpected happens, but that is in most cases a fantasy.

Some mistakes can be fixed quickly if we want them to be. One day our warehouse manager, a woman with a military background who had a tendency to come across as a bit blunt, had an encounter with one of her staff. I happened to run into the coworker shortly after the confrontation, and I saw he was upset.

I went to the warehouse manager to ask if she felt it had gone well with the coworker and if she thought she had been effective.

She said it had not gone well, so I said, "Why don't you restart and try it again so you can say what you really wanted to say and how you wanted to say it?" She did so, and the ineffective situation was improved upon.

Are there any perfect plants, or in reality are all plants perfect in their own way? Why are we so driven to control our organizations when it is an illusion to be able to do so?

One time I had a visit from a study group. One of the participants who ran a car dealership asked me how many people I had reporting to me. Since that was not something I thought of often, I had to count them. The answer was sixteen. The person then asked: "How do you control them all?" My answer to that was simply: "Maybe that is the point! I would never try to control them. I can't even 'control' myself in all situations, so how can I control others?"

No-Cost Budget

"Prediction is very difficult, especially if it's about the future."—Niels Bohr, scientist

Every store in our parent company has to do a huge business plan showing next year's priorities, with all costs broken down into minute detail. Endless hours are spent on this work. In the end everyone is so exhausted that there is a tendency to store this fine document in a nice cupboard!

Sure, a great direction like that of Ford's Alan Mulally, *one Ford*, was most likely broken down into detail at each level in order to be successful. But we believed that anything that couldn't be written down on one page with regard to next year's priorities was unnecessary.

For us the most important thing remained the same year after year: take care of our coworkers and our customers. Everything else was lower in importance.

Another example of our efforts to "keep on rolling" is that we dared to operate from 1994 to 2007 without a cost budget. During that time we enjoyed a cost-percent ratio in relation to sales that was among the best (if not the best) of the stores in the United States every single year.

Not having a cost budget meant we gave our board of directors each year a total store forecast for our profit and loss without splitting up the costs in cost centers. We monitored costs monthly to see if we were pacing toward the total costs forecasted for the full year.

The reason we gave up a detailed cost budget created from the bottom up was that our growth in the first years had exceeded our wildest dreams. It appeared to be a useless exercise to forecast future costs fifteen months in advance (i.e., a cost budget done in March or April before the next fiscal year, which started September 1) while our sales growth was in the 40–60 percent range.

We then realized we could be very cost-conscious without a cost budget. We remained very flexible in upturns as well as downturns. With no budget to stay within or "use up," we simply spent only the money we needed. (After 9/11 and the dot.com crash, corporate had to send out new budget directions. By then we had already adjusted our costs to bring them in line with the sales.)

A prerequisite for the success of such a program is to have constant healthy debates over any spending.

With our local ownership and a strong accounting team, we regularly looked at the most important nonfixed costs, and from time to time we felt the need to bring them back in-line. Overspending was kept to a minimum and would have come with or without a cost budget.

In such a system, coupled with lots of freedom at even the lowest possible levels, one has to constantly take into account what the total cost is for proposed spending.

Pros and Cons of No-Cost Budget

Pros

- Quicker response in upturns and downturns
- More time spent discussing the most important items
- Less total administration time
- Accountability on cost item level
- Focus on actual spending instead of being under or over budget
- "Trains" the managers in healthy fiscal "inquiry"

Cons

- Vagueness
- Unclear how much one can spend
- Unclear who decides what to spend
- Lack of accountability on department level (cost-center level)
- Looks less "professional" on the surface

GENEROSITY

"The more we shared, the better our business seemed to fare."

One of the things my partner and I had decided upon when we started our business was to share if things were going well for us, both with our coworkers and also with our community. It came from a feeling that we truly wanted to share. The way it turned out was that the more we shared, the better our business seemed to fare.

Over thirteen years we were able to do five bonus days for our staff. Bonus days were when we picked a good sales day (always a Saturday, which was our best day of the week) in a solid month (often October) and gave away all the sales from that day to the staff. We also had smaller bonus programs in the years we could not afford the bonus days.

There was no bickering about taking away some costs, like extra staff or advertising etc; the coworkers were simply given all the revenue from that day after tax. Many people thought we were talking about the net profit, but that was not the case. All proceeds before any costs were split among the coworkers according to a formula taking into account seniority and performance. The bonus days not only created surprisingly great PR with our customers and market, but they also showed us how much we really could sell in one day. In each case we sold much more than we believed possible. On the last bonus day on our tenth anniversary, we sold three million dollars' worth of products in one day, which was at that time a world record by a big margin for any store in the chain. Giving back to the community was also incredibly important to us and was always one of our priorities. Our store was one of more than two hundred sister stores, and year after year we gave away far more to our surrounding community than any other store did. In our minds it was still not enough, since the needs that exist in any community are always huge.

Maybe even more important for our culture was the day-to-day generosity. I was lucky to have a partner who was very in tune with what was going on and who was very good at these gestures of generosity. For example, one time a coworker's grandmother was dying of cancer, and her biggest wish was to be allowed to play in our store's play area. This was arranged during after-hours; the woman claimed that this had been one of her happiest moments in life!

Giving away a good mattress to a staff member's terminally ill relative, for example, was another chance to do the right thing. Or allowing and promoting a college fund for a child whose dad (a staff member of ours) had died in an accident. It is never one thing; it is just about doing the right thing over and over whenever situations come up. This also means giving generously when doing internal competitions. A free lunch with the boss was nice, but if someone's efforts had been considerable, we tried to be more generous. A trip to Maui was once the prize, for example.

INFORMAL STRUCTURES

"At the end of the day the organization will live or die depending on the strength and quality of its values. Is this the place where people care to be, where they feel the freedom to follow responsibly what has heart and meaning for them? Do they feel respected, treated with dignity? Is there room for real differences, allowing for innovation?"—Harrison Owen

Most coworkers probably never saw an organization chart of our store. For us a chart seemed to be in contradiction with working together as one team, so we limited concern for structure and who "the boss" was. We found that our way kept the organization "loose" and ready for action.

For the longest time we managed to have only three layers in the store. We saw our organization as three circles.

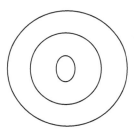

The innermost circle was my partner and I; the next and bigger circle was the other managers; and the last big outer circle was the rest of the staff. Other stores of our size usually had more than eighty managers and at least five layers, whereas we managed with our three layers and forty-two managers. Our flat organization (without too many layers) definitely helped create the culture we wanted to have in our store.

Our track record quickly showed that we were able to create cooperation in our store. We were fostering individuals who were thinking and acting when something needed to be done rather than relying on being told what to do.

We felt that decisions should be made at the level where the most information is at hand. That is generally not at some top manager's level. Our dream was that everyone would feel they were the bosses.

One example was our project groups (more about that later). We chose bright people to lead the planning of very important events throughout the year. Through these roles these coworkers learned how to lead, and in turn we got enthusiastic, energetic projects.

As long as you know whom you report to, what else is there to know? There is a strong tendency among many people to spend more time worrying about their position and if they are doing what they are supposed to be doing instead of identifying what needs to be done and completing the job at hand.

To set the record straight, we were not opposed to people knowing what to do. We did believe in training, buddy systems, task lists, and job knowledge.

What we did not believe in was that by writing very general job descriptions and handing them out, everyone would know what to do. We were very skeptical about the overconfidence we saw elsewhere in companies that used job descriptions.

One of our concerns about the stringent use of job descriptions was that we would create barriers between departments and different jobs. We all had one overriding job description and that was: take care of our customers!

To achieve this, we found that it was very important to split up tasks and make sure everyone knew what was expected of them, but at the same time coworkers should be willing to help out elsewhere if needed. For example, we believed that everyone in our store should know how to serve the customer and use the computer for location information. Everyone should know to pick up paper from the floor or take an abandoned cart from the showrooms, etc.

We also stole an idea from tribes in Africa and elsewhere where the custom is to sit in a ring when meeting. For us it meant that we removed any tables in our conference room and placed the chairs in a large circle in the middle of the room. Sometimes it was even more simple; the participants just stood in a circle. We often used this method when it was important to communicate, i.e. unify a group or come to a consensus.

If it is just information going one way, then the usage of tables is fine. Sure, it is sometimes cumbersome to sit in a ring if you have lots of papers, but you should then ask yourself if you need all those papers to communicate.

One other huge benefit of sitting in a ring is the feeling of equality. The ring causes us to feel as if we are all together and working on equal footing; no one is above or below anyone else. Everyone is important. We also used this technique in our morning meetings in which we would gather and share information, make jokes, and get ready for the day. The social aspect of meetings should not be underestimated.

We chose to call our coordinating group for the whole store, the "Store Group." Other stores call this group "Store Steering Group." Again, it was another way we tried to do everything we could to push our coworkers closest to the issues to take action. So many companies postpone making decisions, needing approval by a management group, board, or special task force. So many decisions are delayed and watered down when they are brought to such groups. There is also a tendency for such groups to overestimate their own importance. We deliberately gave our store group a low profile. It is so easy to push a lot of decisions to such a group so they will then take the blame if something goes wrong.

One time my sister from Sweden was visiting the store. She was proud of her brother and wanted to see my office. I lead her to my desk in the open office, which at that time was the smallest desk we offered, butting up against an equally small desk that my partner used. She said, "Is this all you can get?" I said, "No, I could probably have this whole room as my office, but why would I? I do very little paper work."

In the end I gave up the desk idea totally. And if I needed a place to sit, I moved out to our public restaurant where I could see more coworkers and customers. We tried to be super clear that we really wanted to work very informally.

Another day my youngest son, who was eight at the time, came with me to spend a day at our store, since we were holding a promotion with a famous basketball star whom he wanted to meet. My son followed me around all day, and on the way home he suddenly said: "Dad, you don't do a lot!" I responded, "Come on, I must do something." He answered: "The only thing you do is to go around and talk to staff and then tell the customers where the bathrooms are."

I have told this story many times, creating lots of laughs. He really figured me out! Good thing corporate still thought I did something!

This is what I said at a training class that I gave future store managers in the United States and Canada: "I learned to go overboard in showing our coworkers that I am serious about us as a low-cost and informal company. That means that I will never sit in an enclosed office. I will never have my own computer on my desk. I will never have the biggest desk or the most comfortable chair. I will never have an assistant. I will never have anybody get coffee for me or for my guests. We all have an important job to do, and we do it together."

Every so often my partner and I had a small meeting with all of the recently hired staff. It was called "coffee with Anders and Bjorn" and was a two-hour event where we got to talk about our careers and ourselves and everyone else got to introduce themselves. Since our careers had some ups and downs, most coworkers enjoyed listening to our stories. A few times so many people came that we could not fit enough chairs in a circle in our training room, so my partner and I ended up sitting on the floor.

This would have been quite a strange sight for people coming from companies where the bosses have the big offices and always the best seats!

Speaking of coffee, when my partner and I, along with the management group of corporate, visited the headquarters of Costco, we met Jim Sinegal and Jeff Brotman, the two leading men at this big company. I was very impressed when Jim offered coffee to us and went on to make it himself. That was my kind of guy!

One of the best things I did was when the dishwasher in our restaurant broke down one day: I rolled up my sleeves and started to do the pots!

This area was perceived to be one of the least prestigious in the whole store. I thought nothing of doing dishes for a few hours, but the next few days the news spread across the whole store! What was the big deal? I did dishes at home all the time, so why not in the store? Sometimes we do get chances to show that we really can walk the talk and until then it is only…talk.

At the very start we had hired good managers from other companies. The results were mixed to say the least. We noticed early on that to say that you like an easygoing, casual culture is one thing but to live it is another. One manager coming from a department store chain in southern California was one of the first we had to let go. He was very hardworking and very friendly and cooperative. His main concern was how the big bosses would see him, and this caused him to not always tell the truth or ask for enough help. When I told him he did not "fit" with our culture, he reacted strongly, but after talking to his partner at home, who agreed with me, he realized it was not a good fit for him, either. He was a good person, but not a good fit for our organization.

In another situation we did what we always did, meaning that we asked our staff on the floor what the biggest problem was. This particular day I was told there was a lack of a specific line of bookcases, which was, at that time, our bestselling item in the store. When I asked the lady in charge about this, she told me she did not know why we were out of stock, and then reacted so defensively, I felt obliged to tell her that I was not trying to get her fired, but was just trying to get some bookcases for our customers. Clearly, she was used to only letting the top managers know about the good news and not the bad news.

We once had a great up-and-coming manager who I was especially excited about. I had told him early on that he could come to me and ask questions at any time. One day he came and told me that his supervisor did not seem to want to make him successful since he had not been shown the "paper work"! He had been allowed to lead the work on the floor, but no emphasis had been put on the clerical part of the job.

I assured him that the paper work was the easy part of most managers' jobs, and the hard part was leading a diverse group of people, but he still looked at me a bit skeptically. His view of what a supervisor did and what their priorities were was clearly different from what we tried to promote.

Sometimes it seemed as if we were so different from many other companies, that we were fighting an uphill battle. But the informal culture helped to create a sense of family, to lessen the fear of making mistakes, and reduce the concept of hierarchy.

FUN

"Do the unusual, the unexpected, and don't be afraid to do the Macarena!"

The chapter about our culture would not be complete without some words about the importance of fun. I was lucky to have a partner who was very lighthearted and witty. While I could get caught up in the seriousness of things, he kept injecting humorous remarks along the way. It drove me crazy at times, but it did create an atmosphere of lightheartedness that truly helped our whole culture.

Laughter was commonplace, and doing unusual and fun things was very inspirational for all coworkers. We were only trying to sell some furniture—not performing lifesaving surgery!

The atmosphere also affected our customers and vendors. At one point I was worried about this, since I felt that at the time tax auditors spent too much time with us. They seemed to enjoy our easygoing style. Luckily, we had a fantastic accounting team, so we passed every audit without any glitches, but the auditors did seem to stay for weeks.

Even if our style was easygoing, we always remembered that we were there for our customers. Business had to be taken care of, and we had our fair share of challenges while growing rapidly almost every year.

One time early on, we had long lines at the customer service area. The song "Macarena" came over the loudspeaker, at which point all the staff in the area jumped in and did the dance moves that go with the song. It lightened up an otherwise stressful situation and created lots of laughter.

One practice we implemented was having a morning meeting at the cash registers a few minutes before opening every day.

Everyone stood (to make sure the meeting was short). The supervisors who wanted to come could join us. This was a great place to share last-minute information and even tell a good joke!

The duty manager of the day led the meeting and took notes on anything that needed to be told over the loudspeakers to the rest of the staff. Sometimes we broke out singing to someone in the store who had a birthday to the amusement of the customers who had come early and were enjoying free coffee in the vestibule.

At Christmas we used to play Swedish Christmas music, which drove our coworkers crazy. I was the instigator of it, and after a couple of days of Swedish music, they all had enough. It did create laughter and good conversations, though.

We also tried to do the unusual, the unexpected. We were lucky to work for a company originating from Sweden, and we used our origin to create the unusual. I can't speak of how Swedish companies are doing business in general, but we took the chance to incorporate Swedish traditions into our store. Here are some examples.

Instead of the traditional Christmas party, which takes place when everyone is super busy before Christmas and overdrinking might be a problem, we took on a true Swedish tradition called "Tjugondag Knut", which celebrates the end of Christmas. This takes place in mid-January and is mainly for children.

We danced around a Christmas tree and pretended to throw it out, and each kid got a gift. It was extremely heartwarming to have our coworkers bring their families to this event, which grew and grew over the years. It brought spouses and their children into our "work family."

As the years went by, the party changed into a more diverse children's festival event in which traditions from many different countries were celebrated (though we still kept the name Tjugondag Knut, even if most non-Swedes couldn't pronounce it).

The holiday Lucia is celebrated in Sweden on December 13, so some of us dressed up as Lucia (a young lady in white wearing a wreath crown with candles in it) and "star boys" (wearing a tall, cone-shaped hat), and we "tried" to sing traditional Swedish Christmas songs. This was not a pretty sight, and it was amazing to watch new coworkers see this for the first time. They could not believe the big bosses would make such fools of themselves!

My partner and I used to hand out Christmas gifts to every coworker each year, normally during their shifts. We would interrupt cashiers ringing up a sale with this gift giving. It spread happiness not only to our staff, but to the customers watching.

One of my favorite employees, a fifty-plus-year-old African American man, told me with tears in his eyes that it was the first gift he had ever received from any workplace he had ever been part of!

My partner and I spent numerous hours tracking down each coworker (all six hundred of them). I wore a Swedish Santa mask that was deemed too scary for American kids and even for some of our coworkers, so I had to be discreet about it, and I used it only on special occasions. But it did create lots of laughter, and these moments were among the most fun during the whole year.

Picture 1: Anders Claus, wearing the Swedish Santa mask.

Picture 2: Lucia, getting ready to make fools out of ourselves at the Lucia celebration.

Picture 3: Two official store manager and one unofficial. See chapter University of ...

Picture 4: My partner on clean up duty during one of our off site trainings.

Gardeners

INTRO TO GARDENERS

It is obvious to all of us that a gardener's role is important to the growth of the plants. One is said to have a green thumb when plants are thriving. In our store we could not just hope that someone would have a green thumb. We had to challenge our leaders to work toward achieving that.

The basis for a successful manager/supervisor/area responsible is high job knowledge and good leadership skills. You don't have to be a natural-born leader. Leadership skills can be learned, honed, and improved, just like a good gardener's skills.

Typically, a gardener can do only two things to encourage a plant to grow. He or she can create a good culture or climate (correct temperature, adequate light etc.) and give individual support (the right amount of soil, water, pruning, staking).

It is also commonly known among gardeners that when plants are moved, it takes three years for them to excel. "First year it sleeps, second year it creeps, and third year it leaps."

Compare this to what happens in big companies. Often successful individuals are "uprooted" and then "replanted" in a totally new environment without proper care. This is a survival of the fittest philosophy. It is a quick fix but gives the individual no foundation in the basic values of the company.

We were committed to continuous training of all of our leaders, and we expected them to not only hone their leadership skills, but attend to their own personal growth. They were constantly challenged to let go of ineffective habits and learn to practice more effective ones. As our foundation was, of course, our core values.

Here they are again, to reiterate.

Our Core Values (As Defined by Our Coworkers)

Courage: "Willing to take risks by being open and honest"
Family: "A company and coworkers you can depend on"
Respect: "Treating others fairly and justly with a caring and humble approach"
Initiative: "It is up to you to make it happen."

The following are the qualities we were looking for and that we tried to improve upon. First will come the definitions and then more explanations for each one.

1. Trust: Believe in each person, including yourself, without judgment, restrictions, or control
2. Courage: Take risks by being honest and open
3. Integrity: Lead by example, and practice what you preach

4. Respect: Treat others fairly with a caring and humble approach
5. Vision: See expanded possibilities
6. Enthusiasm: Create a sense of excitement
7. Perseverance: Resolve to finish what we as a company have started
8. Fun: Make room for fun and lightheartedness

Leadership Competencies

Trust: Believe in each person, including yourself, without judgment, restriction or control
The leader:
- Allows coworkers to do their jobs without immediate supervision.
- Respects coworker confidentiality.
- Believes in his/her coworkers.
- Makes the fair decisions for the department and their coworkers.

Courage: Take risks by being honest and open
The leader:
- Is honest and open with his/her coworkers about their performance.

- Take risks and accepts responsibility for the outcomes.
- Continues to learn and grow.
- Shares appropriate information about himself/herself for the benefit of his/her coworkers' learning.

Integrity: Lead by example, and practice what you preach
The leader:
- Walks the talk and practices what he/she preaches.
- Follows basic rules about coming in late, dress code, conduct, etc.
- Is consistent, steadfast, and follows his/her instincts.

Respect: Treat others fairly with a caring and humble approach
The leader:
- Creates an environment where the coworkers feel comfortable going to him/her.
- Treats his/her coworkers fairly.
- Acknowledges and appreciates the contributions of his/her coworkers.

Vision: See expanded possibilities
The leader:
- Shares the vision for the department with his/her coworkers.
- Contributes to the vision of his/her department.
- Encourages coworkers to see the expanded possibilities in the store and company worldwide.

Enthusiasm: Create a sense of excitement
The leader:
- Creates a sense of excitement over what needs to be done.
- Is enthusiastic about getting coworkers involved in learning more about the business.

Perseverance: Resolve to finish what we as a company have started
The leader:
- Encourages his/her coworkers to persevere over obstacles.
- Does not take no for an answer when trying to improve his/her department.

Fun: Make room for fun and lightheartedness

The leader:

- Supports a fun and lighthearted work environment for his/her coworkers.
- Enjoys coming to work.
- Creates and environment where coworkers enjoy working with him/her.

In order for us to know how we were doing in this area, we measured each manager and leader on a yearly basis and gave them feedback on their results. The coworkers of each manager and leader filled out a form. There was also a self-evaluation portion.

SELF-AWARENESS

"When standing in front of a mirror, you see the person you need to get to know better to become a more effective leader."

All of our leadership training was focused on one thing: to increase our leader's self-awareness. We found that it was very hard to be an effective leader and understand others if you did not have some understanding of yourself and awareness of your own feelings, strengths, and what you needed to do to compensate for your own shortcomings.

It is important to know where *you* are in each situation when it comes to your feelings. Some days I came to the store and saw that everyone was grumpy, only to slowly accept that it was me—and not all the others!—who was grumpy.

On days or moments like that, I tried to avoid serious talks with our coworkers, since I felt it would not be fair and I could not be totally there for them.

If I really had to meet with someone, I either took some time for myself or at least was aware of my grumpiness, which for the most part was totally unrelated to the person I was meeting with.

There are many things outside of work that can have a tremendous impact on us, like a sick child at home, financial worries, almost getting into an accident on the way to work, etc.

In the past, when I have asked the very best leaders I know what is most important in becoming more effective as a leader, they've said:

- Self-awareness
- Do not forget yourself—you have to be connected to who you are as a person.
- Be true to who you are, know your strengths, and work to improve.

For many this is easy to say but hard to attain—especially if you are surrounded by people who don't want to hurt your feelings, rock the boat, or give honest feedback.

I've found that the best way to get useful and honest feedback is first to have a trusting culture, and second, to approach the people you work closest with. You also need to be open and ready for whatever feedback could come your way. No excuses!

One very important point in all this is: feedback is not advice! Feedback is what the word says: feeding back what you see without judgment. There are lots of good instruments around to help you analyze yourself, but I have found none better than talking to people around you, providing you trust them and they trust you. They will be the first to notice and support your efforts to make a change (if necessary), especially if you tell them what you are trying to do (see personal plan of action).

It can sometimes be very hard to make radical changes to your attitudes and habits, but for most leaders, all that is necessary is "tweaking" your skills.

I would compare it to an old-time radio with a dial. *If you just make a small adjustment, you can go from noise to wonderful music.*

LEADING BY EXAMPLE

"Growth and comfort do not coexist."—Ginni Rometty, chairman and CEO of IBM

Sometimes we as managers need to take leadership even one step further, like with desks. The more supervising you do, the less paper work you probably have to do, and that means less need for a big desk. As a manager the eyes are on you and your actions. If you do not set the right priorities, you cannot expect others to do the same. This also means that if you spend a lot of time at your desk, you cannot expect your subordinates to do anything different.

People always copy when it is convenient for them. You set the standard with your actions. Do you have to read e-mails first thing in the morning? Is that really the most important thing to do? Or is the sales (or factory) floor more important?

One time a newly appointed store manager from a very traditional country was sent to us for training. On one of the very last days of his training, he came to me and asked if he could discuss a few leadership issues with me since I seemed to have a keen interest in that part of our business.

First he said, "It is really nice of you guys to give each coworker a holiday gift." He then said, "I do things like that too." I was a bit skeptical about this, so I asked him to tell me exactly what he did. He said since it was so warm during the summers in his store, he gave the people on the loading docks cold juice. I was still skeptical, so I asked him again to tell me exactly how it happened. He responded, "I tell my driver to buy the juice, and he gives it to them." I told him that it was a nice idea, but that the process stank! Why did he not do it himself?

After that he asked me how to solve a problem with his office furniture sales manager, who he said always sat at his desk all day.

I then asked what his boss (read: he!) did. The same thing! Sure, he came from a different culture, but I felt he had to do a better job in relating to his coworkers. If you want to get your staff to do something, you'd better be prepared to do it yourself.

As managers we do need to go the extra mile to make ourselves approachable and seen as one of many. Pushing carts, doing dishes when the dishwasher breaks down, wearing the Santa mask, "singing" at Tjugondag Knut, cooking for the staff at gatherings...These are important things when you have a large responsibility. The key is to find things you can do to create the unusual and fortify a bond with your staff.

As managers and supervisors, we are no longer one of the guys, and we have to be aware that all eyes are on us. Drinking too much at team-building events or telling personal stories about alcohol, drugs, sleeping around, etc., is not okay and if you need to vent about something, pick the right listener.

There is a very fine line between going a bit "crazy" at the right moment and crossing that line.

Of course we created lifelong friendships, which led to us socializing with the people we worked with. All this complicates what we can do outside work. The good news is that as long as you do not go totally overboard, you probably will be okay.

Many new managers throw themselves into the details of the job and try their very best to do the "paper work," when it may be more important to "drink coffee with the staff." So instead of doing paper work, meeting every person on the team and finding out about their dreams, ambitions, and concerns should be first on every new manager's agenda.

In the appendix you see how we dealt with boundaries, specifically personal boundaries. There is also another boundary, and that is within the area each coworker can operate. Meaning, what decisions can he/she make? We decided to make our boundaries large and flexible. We wanted to give our coworkers lots of freedom.

We wanted our coworkers to make bold decisions on their own without checking with a "boss," and to take risks and assume the responsibilities that followed each risk. Many managers make this part very small and very controlled. We did not wish to do the same.

Compare this situation to that of a gardener. If a gardener puts a strong plant in a very small pot, the plant will soon will die. It will suffocate in the small pot, or it will adapt to a small pot environment and not learn to take risks or grow. We set our plants in a pot just a bit too big so we could enjoy the incredible growth that would ensue.

CONFRONT WITH LOVE!

"It is about a respectful feedback on what we see."

One of the biggest contributors to the incredible growth of many of our leaders was how we dared to "confront them with love." It seems like there is a fear in most companies to give their employees honest feedback about what they see.

This is not about judging, criticizing, or complaining about an individual. It is about respectful feedback on what a leader notices, like holding up a mirror and talking with a coworker about what you see.

It is more about asking questions than giving answers. In many companies it seems to be more about judging and rating different traits.

One of the ways we gave feedback was to ask coworkers to draw pictures of how they saw themselves in the organization on that day. After a ten-minute drawing, we would look at the picture together and ask the coworker questions instead of making statements. It was amazing how much discovery came out of these sessions.

The ones who were able to honestly work on their discoveries seemed to catapult their careers to a higher level. They appeared in the end more stress-free and positive. The hard part for everyone was to make the adjustment. It meant leaving old habits and attitudes and learning new ones, but of course the longer one has had old habits, the harder they are to change. I used to say that I spent more than fifty years with some of my habits, and it was very hard to say farewell to them.

We did notice that the longer an individual had spent in a strict controlling environment (unfortunately, that covers most big companies today), the harder it was for him or her to trust our environment and make the necessary adjustments.

We had tremendous success with homemakers who returned to work after having children. They knew everything about chaos and adapted easily to our sometimes-chaotic environment. They seemed to have nothing to defend, and several of them became good leaders. In many of those cases our only job was to help them see their own potential.

For others it seemed impossible to make the necessary changes. You can compare this to a gardener having a plastic plant. On the surface it looks good, but no matter how much water or fertilizer you give it, it will not change. It is important not to waste all your energy on trying to get these plastic plants to grow. Of course, this is one of the hardest things for a manager to understand: when to stop and let go of a plastic plant.

As a manager I needed a lot of time to reflect on these tough situations. Often I would get up in the middle of the night and write a letter about what I felt. If I still felt the same in the morning, I would act upon whatever it was. If not, I would discard the letter.

I sent one of those letters early on in my career to someone who did not get a very senior job she had applied to. The circumstances were such that I was unable to give the news in person. I have always felt that I express myself better in writing than over the phone, so I decided to write a fairly long letter explaining the decision. This person was a good coworker, and years later we later offered her a job in our store. Two weeks before she was to arrive to discuss the details of her employment, she was in a quite serious car accident. Fortunately, she had limited injuries, but not only was her car wrecked, her day planner and all its contents had flown out of the car, save one thing: the letter I had written to her four years earlier. It had somehow gotten stuck and was recovered.

When we finally met, I got a chance to reread the letter. Evidently, there was something in it that had struck a chord and she had saved it for so many years. We looked at it together, and even if there were some strong learning points in it, it also contained lots of love.

For many of us, it is hard to see the love at first. We tend to concentrate on the "learning points." In the end this coworker decided not to accept the job due to unrelated personal reasons. But I was happy to reconnect, and she still helped us a lot with comments and advice in regards to our displays.

FIRE WITH LOVE!

"Use Tai Chi first, then if that does not work, go to Aikido, and as last resort, use Karate."

"Who is coming?" I asked. On a regular store visit early on in my career I was told that a former employee wanted to see me. This was a person I had let go two years earlier, and I felt as if I could have handled the situation better. So what did he want from me? I hope he is not bringing a gun, I thought to myself.

But there he was with a big smile and a few more pounds, giving me a bear hug and thanking me for letting him go.

He was now a baker instead of a manager in a retail store, and he was much happier. It does not always work out so well each time I let someone go, but for me this was when I realized that things are not always exactly as I might imagine they are.

Letting a coworker go was one of the most dreaded and thankfully not so common tasks I had as a leader. At first I made the mistake of letting anger or irritation build up inside me, and then I would have to talk to the coworker in question. Sure, there are often disappointments involved on both sides, and sometimes, for whatever reason, things do not always work out as hoped for.

In situations in which plant closures or employee theft are not the case, it is often not a black-and-white situation. One day I had to let a young lady go due to too many attendance issues, but it was still hard to let an otherwise excellent employee go. From that moment on I changed the way I looked at these situations.

Sometimes people are begging us to let them go in their own peculiar way. This person had voted with her feet many times, telling us that she did not want to be there. It was time for me to release her, to let her go.

During our talk she blamed her car, her boyfriend, the traffic, but then I asked her if she would be at the airport on time if she had won a two-week, all-expenses-paid trip to the Bahamas.

She said of course she would. I responded that until she saw her work as a trip to the Bahamas, we would have to part company. Years later she came into the store as a customer and thanked me for teaching her a good life lesson.

Another time I had to let a cash manager go. Instead of telling him what I thought was wrong with him, I just asked him one simple question: "Are you happy here?" He said: "No, I feel like a dad to our thirty cashiers, and I already have enough kids at home." I responded: "So our task here and now is to make sure you can leave here in a good way." Instead of an angry person, I again got a hug and thanks.

I used to have an old Swedish car (being originally from Sweden). The car was great when it worked, but it seemed as if there was often something wrong with it. So when I had to let another good coworker go due to attendance issues, I told him, "You are just like my Saab: I don't know if you will perform today or not. So I have to let you go."

This analogy became so popular among other managers that several employees were likened to my Saab when they were let go.

So after some bad and some decent (they are never really good) firings, this is what I learned:

- Always show respect, because who are you to say that you know how it is to be in another person's shoes? I called it "fire with love."
- Make it short—max five minutes. After you have made the decision, there is not much else to talk about. This is not the time to argue about shortcomings; just be clear with your reasons for firing and that's that.
- To give feedback when you are angry is always wrong. Choose a time and place when you are at ease. Be generous in your settlement. If you are not generous, the rest of the staff will find out and it will cost you more in the long run.
- The rest of the staff, no matter how discreet you are, will always watch a letting go. It will impact your company culture if you don't deal with low performers or accept the odd honest mistakes. I find it amazing that

companies still believe in fear tactics. Remember: respect is the key word.

- It is important to do your homework and let people know early about lack of performance. How respectful is it to let a low performer believe they are doing a good job and then let them go shortly afterward?

- We always tried to use as little force as possible when dealing with our coworkers. Our motto was to use Tai Chi first, then if that does not work, go to Aikido, and as a last resort, use Karate. Close attention was paid to how we sat, whether we were really present, and how we approached the coworker.

It all has to be done with the outmost respect. In a garden center it is quite natural for all plants not to make it. Some do not thrive, and this is nothing to get upset over - even if it is not fun to see a good plant fade away. We realized that our garden center was not perfect for everyone.

TEAM LEADERSHIP

"Our world is very complex; just ask any single parent how hard it is to do it alone."

One of the most asked questions my partner and I got over our thirteen years as co-managers was: who does what in between the two of us? Tell us exactly who does what, so there is no confusion.

We never got why this was so important, and we never worried about it. We were in effect two equal partners and two equal store managers.

From the beginning we had a vague idea that my partner would work more toward the outside (marketing, press, and customer service), and I would work more internally (human resources, operations and finance).

We realized after a while that it actually worked without rules and definitions. We just made up some basic rules of conduct:

- If an employee asks one of us a question and gets an answer, that answer will stand no matter what the other partner thinks (to avoid the "ask Mom if Dad says no" syndrome).
- It was up to us to inform the other one about all important dealings, especially with regard to coworkers.
- My partner handled all marketing, press, and customer service, and I handled HR and finance. The rest we shared, but each of our managers had one of us as a main manager to turn to.
- Was it confusing for the staff? Sometimes I am sure it was, and even if one of us could have run the store on our own, the team approach was key to our success. Together we were a strong team that was able to offer very good leadership.
- In today's more and more complex world, we felt that this setup was the best for all. Most of us never ask our parents (provided we are

lucky enough to have both around) who is really in charge. Somehow each issue is dealt with over time. Our world is very complex; just ask any single parent how hard it is to do it all alone.

- We rolled out our team leadership model to many of our departments with more success than failure. When it worked, it was a tremendous tool to place a younger manager side by side with a more experienced one to create a seamless change should one of them be promoted somewhere else in the organization. When it did not work, it almost always had to do with ineffective managers.

The first team leadership (other than my partner and I) model started when we had to get rid of one of our managers and had no one who could take over without strong supervision. We had two senior coworkers, one with more skill but who was sometimes a bit rough on staff, and one who was softer and more successful with staff but maybe not so knowledgeable about the job, so we decided to let them lead the department together.

I cannot say it turned out perfectly, but it was successful enough to inspire us to arrange for more team leadership positions. At one time all major positions in the store were filled by two people. It allowed us to handle leadership changes easily when we were growing quickly.

I loved this concept very much, especially for an organization that has many hours of operation. The standard hierarchy in most companies is one main manager and one assistant manager. Our setup included two equal managers. The difference is small but important. It's mostly in the feeling and perception for both managers and coworkers.

Decisions can be made by either manager more quickly (one manager's job was to inform the other about any decisions), and each manager was forced to operate with another person.

I really believe it sped up each manager's development. And it not only gave each manager a close partner to bounce all ideas off of and come to agreements with, but it also created a bit of competition. For those who saw the benefits, they really thrived. For those who did not, they seemed less flexible, less capable of handling chaos, and in need of more control.

The people from our store who now have the best careers in the parent company were all part of team leadership at one time. Coincidence? No, I don't think so.

On the note of teams, I was early in my career when I faced leading a group of sixteen store managers and senior staff. I tried with no success to get all sixteen to agree to each of our actions. I believed I had to get everyone on board to make things happen. Later I realized that as long as I had most people with me, we could still create success.

There will always be people who love to steal the limelight under the pretense of being the devil's advocate. Sure, it is important to listen to all concerns before you set out, but after that it is important just to make it happen! Many of those hesitant people will jump on board when they see the process start.

You can liken it to a still pond. If you throw a big rock in the middle, it will create waves. If then several more rocks are thrown in at the same place, it reinforces the waves, and in the end they will reach the shore, strong and firm. That is how you want the process to happen.

Compare this to when rocks (read: opinions, devil's advocate) are thrown in everywhere, eliminating the first rock's waves. It will create choppy water and confusion within the organization.

In a gardener's world, this occurs when he or she tries to grow too many plants in the same small area. This tactic will create many weak little plants and probably none that are big and strong enough to sell.

PROJECT GROUPS

"Give people a chance to take charge, and you will be rewarded by seeing them, and your business, grow."

Every store has events that reoccur each year. In our case these events were our twice-a-year sales event; our catalog drop in August; our Christmas event; and a few others. Each event was so large, it needed special attention, and every store manager chaired these events to bring them to a successful completion.

We saw these events as a great learning opportunity, so we formed project groups for each event and we phased ourselves out of these groups.

We realized that there was much more enthusiasm for the events if there were constantly new people involved in planning to make them the best ever.

For a store manager leading the Christmas event for the twenty-seventh time, there is little new and exciting for him/her.

We realized this was a chance for new leaders to test their abilities, to grow, and to learn to handle bigger tasks. To minimize financial risks for us, we implemented a rule that you had to be the vice chair in at least one event before you could lead an event on your own. We also insisted on taking minutes at event meetings and keeping them in special binders so old lessons could be looked at to minimize future mistakes.

This became a huge success for us. It fostered many good new leaders who would have otherwise had to wait maybe years before they could show their abilities. And the project leaders got to pick their own teams, thus learning how to pick good players. Sometimes the nicest people are not the ones you can rely on in difficult situations.

I SEE YOU...! I AM HERE!

"I am not going to treat you players all the same. Giving you the same treatment doesn't make sense because you're all different."—John Wooden, American basketball player and coach

During our many training sessions, we often heard "I want to be liked" from our new managers. Our response was always that to be liked by your coworkers is a farfetched dream. When most of us do not even like ourselves all the time, how can we then think other people will always like us? They might like some things about us, but certainly not everything.

I have seen this story in several books about how members in a tribe in Africa greet one another when they meet. The meeting goes like this:

"I see you!"

"I am here!"

To be "seen" is maybe all we can hope for. Interestingly, the word respect comes from the Latin word *respicere*, which means "look at, regard, consider." *Respicere* itself is a combination of two words re ("I") + specere ("look"), hence the word for "glasses," spectacles.

So if we combine the two words, we can say that the only thing we really can strive for as supervisors is to earn respect from our coworkers—that they will see us!

One other strong ambition among new managers is to be "nice." We used to say that "niceness" does not cut it! In our efforts to be "nice," we often confuse niceness with accepting less than good efforts. We tend not to say anything and hope problem situations will go away. Sometimes they do, but there is nothing nice about not confronting a not-so-good performer, and sooner or later someone will have to deal with it. And, unfortunately, there is sometimes a tendency to ship these low performers to an unsuspecting colleague responsible for another department.

There is a world of difference between having a positive view of everyone and treating them with utmost respect, and accepting bad performance. To be nice by omission should not be confused with direct, open, and honest feedback.

In every group there will be high and low performers, and a supervisor's most difficult task is to know when to step in and get rid of low performers. People go through ups and downs in life, and we sometimes really have to wait for previous good performers to hopefully return to their old selves. The big question is how long you should wait. That will depend on the organization, how important that person is to the whole, and of course what is causing the sudden low performance.

To talk about things openly with the person involved is the best way to handle these types of situations. We were royally rewarded by sticking it out with some of our people. This is one of the most difficult tasks for a supervisor. Again, niceness does not cut it! Instead set the stage for growth!

"How do you motivate your staff?" This was a frequent question from both new managers and people seeing our success from the outside. I had a hard time answering this question at first, since I felt and still feel that motivation comes from within. To say you can motivate someone indicates that you have control over that person.

Just as a gardener really cannot make plants grow exactly as he wants them to, we as leaders cannot force our coworkers to grow exactly as we want them to. What you can do is to set the stage for growth. A gardener can make sure his or her plants have the right amount of soil, fertilizer, and water, and ensure that the conditions in the greenhouse are ideal. The gardener has to pay attention to each plant and moderate the above "support" in order to obtain growth. Not every plant grows the same way and under the same conditions. Some plants might have to be moved to enhance their growth.

All this is not very different from what a leader can do. We can certainly set the stage for growth by having the right expectations and incentives for a coworker. Many managers think that money is the only motivator for growth, but I happen not to believe this. Money is one of many incentives, but most are nonmonetary. At the outset our job was to show possibilities, "hold up the mirror" to show that we believed the person could grow, and reinforce a coworker's strength by pointing out growth possibilities. Our job was to pay attention to the person both at the start and throughout the process.

Motivation is an inside job, meaning that the person has to unleash his or her own drive for growth and performance. Given the right stage, my experience is that most people do have the ability to grow and excel. Our store and our retail environment were not the right stage for everyone, so some people went on to other things.

Timing might also have been wrong for certain individuals; they were not ready to grow.

Something else that was not visible for us had to grow inside them before they could take a step we could see.

Obviously, some people do not want to grow or change, and they get stuck at the same place, which in our case normally meant that they would leave the company. It is important to recognize that in terms of growth, we did not mean for all coworkers to aspire to become formal leaders. What we did ask was that everyone work to support our culture. Many people feel that growth only comes if you get a new job. I disagree. We tried to open up many possibilities for everyone to take part in project groups, committees etc. We also instituted a work rotation program.

We even had a special task group we called flex force. These coworkers were trained in almost all jobs around the store and could jump in wherever needed. Our culture was such that we wanted to be open to change and inspire growth.

Just as the gardener pays attention to his plants and makes adjustments, we as leaders need to switch channels in our leadership if one way of working proves ineffective.

In our case that meant we gave a coworker new tasks to do, or we even changed a coworker's department as a very last resort, provided we really believed in that coworker's growth potential.

The most effective tactic seemed to be when a supervisor changed his or her own way of dealing with an individual, such as by paying more attention to the coworker. Often the expectations had not been expressed clearly.

I used to say, if you don't believe in your own staff, who will? I had little tolerance for managers who came to me to complain about their staff. It was their staff, and they had often hired them. They had to deal with them. If they needed support, we would be there. Some people are harder to inspire than others.

Our job was to keep switching channels until we saw success. Many managers think it is up to employees to make adjustments to a certain managerial leadership style. We found that it was much more effective if the leaders were attuned to their coworkers, just like a good gardener would be to his plants.

LEADERSHIP AND PERSONAL DEVELOPMENT TRAINING

"The only way to put good leadership into practice is to...practice!"

For many organizations, training either means bringing in an expensive consultant to fix a problem, letting HR take care of it, or just leaving everyone to fend for themselves with on-the-job training. For us it was different. Training became a way of operating, a way of leading, and quite simply a way of being.

Since our growth happened so fast, we often had people in new leadership positions. Our experience was that after a relatively brief honeymoon period in which staff and a leader all seemed to be very positive, a period of more "somber and critical" thinking arrived. It seemed that people noticed more flaws with the new situation.

Our job was to help our leaders through this period. If we were successful, the leaders and staff alike seemed to be more at ease.

Our training was critical in helping new leaders overcome the somber period and learn more skills in handling their staff better. You can compare it to a new plant in a new environment. It does well at first when replanted, but then it has an adapting period. Not all plants make it through this change, and it is the same with some leaders.

We can't over exaggerate the importance of training in our success. The benefits we received were on so many levels. We created better leaders and more motivated staff, improved chances for internal promotions, and foremost incited a sense in the store that we really cared about our staff. Our belief was that leadership skills are something that can be learned. They are not something you are just born with. These skills can be enhanced by practice, just like any other skill can. The training was there for the participants to learn new skills and have a safe environment for practicing.

From the start, long before we knew we would be successful as a store, we were committed to leadership training. In the end we were taking around one hundred people (20 percent of all staff) away to annual trainings. This included not only our managers, but also our hourly paid area responsibles and trainees.

On top of that, we ran yearlong training classes for smaller groups, as well as biannual follow-ups with everyone who had attended the away-from-store training. All training was on a voluntary basis, and we actually had one or two managers choose not to attend. There were no hard feelings about that since it also helped to show that participation truly was voluntary.

The cost of this training was ridiculously low in comparison to the impact; say 0.1 percent of all sales. Without fail, we could feel a buzz in the store during and after each training. It came from all the good people who got the chance to run the store when the "big" managers were away. After the training the buzz came from everyone feeling a sense of hope and determination to work together even better as a team.

I used to have a saying that played on my imperfect English: "I can't learn you anything," meaning that we all have to do our own learning. It is up to us to do our utmost to learn in all situations. In English the words for learning and teaching are very different. I can teach someone a lot, but we all have to do our own learning!

There is no question that we insisted people would be learning if they chose to attend the trainings. The climate in the store was made for learning. If you did not learn, you wasted your time there, whether you intended to stay there for a long time or for a short time while you figured out what you wanted next in life.

Our aim was to constantly bring our leaders out of their comfort zones to help them stretch into more of a learning zone. Most of our training was experiential. Too often training is focused merely on taking information into your head.

We found it more effective to challenge ourselves and really put into practice what we learned right away.

Most of our training was aimed at increasing self-awareness. While we sometimes ran the training ourselves, we did often bring in some excellent consultants to take us further.

Since our business was so full of people, both coworkers and customers, we also spent a lot of time working to improve our communication skills. Some of our leadership training took place off-site. We tried to find places where we could do all the cooking ourselves. The participants were divided into teams for cooking, table setting, and cleanup. Not only did this reinforce our family atmosphere, it fostered a sense of camaraderie. If there were slackers, they would stand out like sore thumbs and correct their behavior next time.

PERSONAL PLANS OF ACTION

"Hold everyone's feet to the fire!"

Most organizations do trainings, and then hope for the best that the trainings will lead to the necessary changes. We never wanted to take that risk, so we came up with personal plans of action. We wanted to ensure trainings were not just great experiences but would lead to long-term results and continuity between sessions. Therefore, each leader had to commit to a personal plan for improvement, which would be followed up on every six months until a new plan was written.

We formed small groups during the follow-ups in which we went through everyone's statements and reviewed their work. Since the statements had to be something visible, it was possible for the closest coworkers to know if a person had worked on his or hers.

I can't remember a situation in which a coworker said he or she had worked on it and no one had seen it. It was very obvious whether someone had worked on the necessary change. Of course, the situations were uncomfortable at times, but we all understood that change is sometimes very hard to achieve.

The following are actual statements from a group of area responsibles. These statements were shared with all leaders so we could better support one another in our respective growth.

- I need to open up and speak to the person as soon as possible when an issue arises.
- I need to work on being more assertive in my communication and leadership.
- I need to more forcefully enlist the cooperation of people to succeed at urgent, important, and doable tasks.
- I need to be a better listener and give more helpful instructions and feedback based on the situation.
- I need to be gentler with coworkers instead of thinking that they know exactly what I am thinking.

- I need to be less controlling and relax in the knowledge that the job will get done and I don't always have to do it by myself.

- I need to realize that the people around me may not know what is expected of them and to be more firm in communicating what it is that I expect.

- I need to be more aware and understanding of my coworkers.

- I need to improve my ability to initiate contact with a coworker when I need to confront them.

- I need to get to the root of each problem and address it professionally.

- To be a better communicator, I must clarify and identify the real "hot point" in order to work to resolve it.

- I need to work on my listening skills and body language.

- I need to work on listening and allowing people to come to their own conclusions.

- I need to be more clear and direct with my instructions and expectations.

- I need to talk more, express my needs, and be more assertive.

- I need to address a potential situation before it becomes a problem.
- I need to work on letting others know how I feel before I hit a boiling point.
- I need to be more specific with details when giving directions so that my coworkers understand what I mean and I don't have to double-check the work given.

Our Plants

Intro to Our Plants

What is growth? For plants it looks pretty simple, but is it so? Do we know what branches should grow next? Do we know how tall a plant will be and how long it will keep growing?

We defined personal growth as "a person's ability to change in a way that will enhance his or her contribution to the whole". In nature, untouched by humans, harmony exists in each system, and growth does not necessarily mean "bigger. In business one can often see growth without quality when several big companies are merged under one umbrella and exist without contributing to the whole. It seems we try to force growth without success.

How successful is the gardener who yells at his plants to grow faster or over fertilizes them? It is obvious that a gardener can do only two things to "make" plants grow. He or she can create a climate of growth and give support to individual plants.

Support for a plant includes the right soil, the right amount of water, the right amount of fertilizer, and individual care such as removing dead leaves, etc. The climate of growth is characterized by maintaining the correct temperature and level of sunlight.

Since we opened our store, we saw many people join us and experience incredible personal and professional growth. At the same time, many smart, hardworking individuals came and went without experiencing this growth. We, of course, realized that retail was not for everyone. But our ambition was to make sure we took care of all talent that came to us, whether a coworker's intention was to have a long-term career or to just make some money while deciding what to do next.

In Daniel Coyle's book *The Talent Code: Greatness Isn't Born, It's Grown. Here's How.,* he talks about three things that create talent: deep practice, ignition, and master coaches.

First let's see what we did for deep practice. Our motto was to constantly strive to become better leaders.

But to become good, you need to get feedback on how you are doing.

We did this through confronting with love, a process by which our leaders found out how they were doing. Our training was focused on putting into practice the things we learned as soon as we could and to do them over and over until we got good at them.

Our personal plans of action with feedback sessions helped lay out the route for each leader. Daniel Coyle writes: "What would be the surest method of ensuring that LeBron James started clanking jump shots, or that Yo-Yo Ma started fudging chords? The answer: don't let them practice for a month."

It is clearly not enough to read a book about leadership or listen to a great speech. We need to practice being good leaders and to make what we learn "stick" over and over. Yes, we were pushy to get our leaders out of their comfort zones, but the results in the end were better leaders.

The second element in growing talent according Daniel Coyle is ignition.

With all our trainings, and the participation of twenty percent of all our coworkers in said trainings, we created a culture of growth. Growth was what we expected: Personal and company growth.

We constantly looked for it, and as some of our leaders said "someone believed in me and held up a mirror so I could see my own potential."

The third element in Daniel Coyle's book is master coaching. He says: "Their personality—their core skill circuit—is to be more like farmers: careful, deliberate cultivators. They're down-to-earth and disciplined."

I don't think any of us saw ourselves as master coaches, but we certainly saw ourselves as gardeners. We saw incredible growth and became energized when growth occurred. To fail once in a while was accepted and expected. It was part of the growth process, but we constantly tried to become better at what we were doing, by adapting till we got success. Coyle also writes: "Patience is a word we use a lot to describe great teachers at work. But what I saw was not patience, exactly. It was more like probing, strategic impatience.

The master coaches I met were constantly changing their input. If A didn't work, they tried B and C; if they failed, the rest of the alphabet was holstered and ready."

THE UNIVERSITY OF OUR STORE

"Our plants were growing nicely!"

Here is an example of our efforts to entice our coworkers to grow: an actual article from our monthly newsletter written in 2002.

"An ex-coworker wrote to me this week:
You should really call the store a university for all the incredible learning that takes place there. Thank you for allowing me to make mistakes and still have a job. I have grown in so many ways because of my experience with the store, but I wish I had been more focused and purposeful with my time there, and that I had made myself promotable earlier.

I cannot tell you how happy I was to receive this letter, despite the pain of losing a great person. A lot of what we worked for is covered in those few sentences.

We want to make the time every coworker spend with us worthwhile and at the same time sell lots of furniture and hopefully create a better everyday life for many people through our great products and incredible prices.

If everyone who works in a store could see it as a sort of university where we all learn every day to better prepare ourselves for what is next for us in life, whether it is a long-term career here or elsewhere, then we could make it an even better place to spend the major part of our days.

Now here is a question for you: What are you doing with your time? Are you filling up time, or are you learning as much as you could? Even if your dream is to become a teacher, a pilot, a policeman, or a doctor, you can learn skills in this company that you will be able to use in those professions. In almost all jobs you will have to deal with people, and we do that often in our store. You can also learn how to take on more responsibility, how to plan, how to sell, etc.

You can here learn skills here that you can use everywhere.

For example when we had the flood during our remodel. I came in just before nine and found everyone working that morning mopping up water and trying hard to get prepared to be able to open the store at 10:00 a.m. That is when I like our store the most! We almost take it for granted that we pull together and are not concerned over who was to blame. But the contractor, who was not yet used to us, came to me and said: "Fire me!" My answer was: "Why would we do that? Anybody can make mistakes, but how you react now is how I can tell if you are good or not." I must say that everyone did well. I had never seen so many blowers in my life. Not only does the way we work in our store have on impact on ourselves, but it impacts the suppliers and customers around us! If you tell me this would have happened in most places of business, I would say you are wrong.

For the record I do feel we have many, many here who have realized that this is a place of learning.

Freedom with responsibility is not just an empty phrase. I also know that the way we work is not for everyone. I hope I can encourage anyone who works here to take good care of the time you have at the store and to make the most of it even if you are not sure if it is your long-term career. "

The idea is to try to eat the elephant bit by bit, meaning, don't decide your whole life in one go. I for sure never knew what I wanted to do with my life, but every step I took felt very right at the time. If you feel your career is not working out as you want it to, please talk to your manager, and if you are still not sure what to do, talk to myself or Bjorn. We will be happy to do what we can to help you.

"Keep learning and selling!"—Anders"

At one time all the store managers from southern California visited our store. After two days of intensive scrutiny, they gave us their report, which was as follows: "We don't think your store looks any better than any of our stores, but you are so lucky—your staff is so nice!" The first feeling was one of disappointment, but then we realized that this was what we had been trying to achieve. We had a great staff, and we were crazy enough to believe that we had something to do with it. Our plants were growing nicely!

Nothing of what was accomplished would have been possible if not for our tremendous group of coworkers. I can't say we were exceptional in our hiring practices (we did vary between fifteen percent staff turnover per year to more than forty percent during the "booming" economy years), but after a while we had a core group of dedicated, courageous learners for whom no task was too big or impossible.

Some of the newly hired coworkers stuck with us and joined the core group, while others moved on to other jobs.

It seemed like the store took on a life of its own where one success lead to another.

Our job was to constantly look ahead and not dwell on our mistakes. We had to remodel our store five times to handle the growing business.

One story typical for how the culture was in our store goes like this: early on we had hired a lady over sixty. She was going to stay with us for just a short while to make some money for a trip she wanted to take. She ended up staying with us for ten years! One day my partner and I walked through the store when we happened to run into her. She came up to us and said with a glint in her eyes: "All three of us are here today." (Indicating humorously that she was saw herself as a store manager too). After that we called her the third store manager. She was in no formal leadership role but became a leader in the store in her own way. Whenever she found us doing something, she would poke some fun at us and quickly comment: "I am glad to see you're finally working!" We had many examples like this.

It is clear to me that by being very respectful to every, and I mean every employee, they responded by making the store their own.

We lived through the ups and downs of our coworkers' lives. Many companies see their staffs as a resource among many others. We saw ours as friends, providers of our success, and our extended family.

There were many moments of truth, but I can find no better example than when it was 10:00 p.m. and closing time, and a tired coworker had their partner sitting in the car waiting for them outside, and they still continued to satisfy a customer's need and even offered to add on items like a mattress to the bed, chair pads for the chairs, etc. I am sure it did not happen all the time, but it happened enough to make our sales grow. We showed our customers that we cared about them even at or past closing time.

The store seemed to belong to the whole staff, and they were proud to work there. On top of that, the majority of our managers had either started as full-time or part-time staff somewhere in the store.

Very few had been managers before they came there. The time it took for them to become managers varied from a year to several years depending on the individual and the opportunities.

At the same time, the path of succession is not always clear. There can be some confusion about what to do at certain points. But when we reach such obstacles, here is where each of us needs to take on extra responsibility. When situations are cloudy, the coworker has to take it upon himself or herself to ask questions and work to clarify them. Paths aren't always clearly marked or cleared of brush for an easy walk. Everyone must do their parts to make their path.

What do we mean by growth, anyway? We define personal growth as "a person's ability to change in a way that will enhance his/her contribution to the whole." Growth in a store might look like taking on more responsibilities, such as becoming an area responsible or a project leader, taking part in training, assuming responsibility when no one else does, speaking up, suggesting improvements, etc. What we as leaders can do is to set the stage and create the ideal climate. It will then be up to the individual to make it happen!

We provided many opportunities in our organization.

Like our numerous training programs, our different way of running our big projects, our flat organization, and our trainee-program, that gave everyone plenty of chances to grow and practice.

Learning becomes especially beneficial to our growth when it goes further than cramming more facts into our brains, particularly when learning "touches" us so deeply that it increases our awareness about ourselves.

A very normal career path for our managers looked something like this:

- Start as full-time or most probably part-time
- Excel at what you do and decide to make a go at a career in our company
- Apply to become an area responsible
- Apply to our trainee program (called Aspirant)
- Apply to a manager job, probably for a smaller department
- Apply to MAST (Management and Supervisor Training) program
- Take on a larger department and take part in yearly leadership training

RECOVERY

"Watch out for waste: both resources and time!"

Not long after we opened our store, we hired a man who called himself a "misfit". After some time he was appointed manager of our "as is" department, where we sold scratched or dented items at reduced prices. The department was later renamed the "recovery department."

Early on the whole store was so enthused by our way of working that they started to find ways, on their own, where we could save. One example was that they put up a huge sign over our compactors that nothing could be thrown away without me or my partner present. They had become upset over all the "good stuff" that was thrown away and felt we needed to do something about it.

This eventually led to a proposal from the recovery manager to take the idea to a whole new level.

We started a program to not only save perfectly good pieces of the best sellers, but also invested in machinery by which one of his staff could repair items that had been broken in handling or from being used by our fifty thousand customers per week. Most items in the store were put under more stress in one week than during a lifetime of normal use in a person's home.

We worked out a system where we started to keep an inventory of parts for our most popular items. We could then, instead of opening a box with a perfectly good item to retrieve, say a side piece, to satisfy a customer bringing in a broken side piece, check our inventory of parts and give the customer the needed part without having to open a new box and discard whatever the customer did not need.

Sounds pretty simple and logical, right? The work was in keeping relevant inventory, which most stores at the time felt was unnecessary or too much work. But our calculations showed that the payback of any occurred expenses was immense.

My partner and I were a bit reluctant about the idea at first, but this man would not take no for an answer. And I hate to admit it, but he got my partner's vote first, and together they worked on me. It was a very sizeable investment in machinery at that time.

But this program ended up saving us hundreds of thousands of dollars locally every year, and later, when it was taken to the parent company, the impact was millions of dollars saved worldwide. (To my knowledge we were the only store buying machinery, but the other stores did the inventory systems). At first the parent company was reluctant, but after we had carried this man's expenses traveling around for a some months, the controllers started to see the results and hired him.

We also got another huge benefit from investing in the machinery. Sometimes, due to supply problems, we could not get bed slats for our beds. We then started to produce the bed slats ourselves. This enabled us to continue to sell beds, which otherwise would have been impossible without this vital part.

Thousands of dollars in lost sales were avoided, and the part was easy and safe to produce ourselves, though it was probably not what we wanted the parent company to find out about. But we believed our job was to satisfy our customers first and foremost.

Not only is this a huge success story financially, but it is also a prime example of the freedom and trust we gave to our coworkers. We had a department that we were incredibly proud of, a staff whose members took their jobs to a different level. The whole store became involved in recycling, saving, and minimizing our loads to the landfill. We avoided sending thousands of pounds of waste to the landfill. It made sense environmentally, financially, and morally.

Another example of minimum waste was our restaurant. Thanks to the inspiration of the leadership in that department, we managed to have a considerably higher gross profit than any other sister restaurant. This was due to great planning and care in avoiding waste.

INTERNAL PROMOTIONS

"Homegrown fruit and vegetables always seem to taste better."

To promote from within makes sense for most companies, but it still does not seem to happen as much as it should. The argument against it is often simply that no one is ready.

Also, the grass always seems to be greener on the other side, meaning a person from the outside appears more competent than someone whose shortcomings you know well. My partner and I were given chances far beyond what we were ready for early in our careers, but we rose to each challenge. Did we make mistakes? Sure, many, but we learned from them. We were therefore determined to give the same opportunity to as many of our coworkers as we could.

Other than our start-up, we did not hire a manager from the outside. Over the years we lost most of the managers we had hired in the beginning. Some transferred to other stores while some went to other companies.

In late 2006 we welcomed a team of corporate specialists who conducted a regular check that all stores have to go through, and after twelve years of operation, it was found that 92 percent of our managers had come from within. We were told they had never seen a number that high in any other store. It was never our ambition for us to do it this way; it just worked out like that. We were very proud of it.

Our total dedication was to give our coworkers the chance to grow through on-the-job training, area responsible training, and leadership training, and it was paying off. Every year we got more and more applicants for each area responsible and manager position.

It is important to note that it is not enough to give someone a chance; it is our responsibility to set up a person for success. The area responsible (AR) system proved invaluable to getting a better look at who would succeed in a manager role. With more than fifty ARs, we had plenty of chances to see who was best suited for a bigger role.

It is extremely important not to promote someone simply because someone has paid his or her dues or has been an AR for a long time. You do not do anyone any favors by giving someone a chance despite serious doubts. It is much better to have the tough talks before—not after—someone becomes a manager.

We had always been good at involving several managers in the few decisions about letting someone go, but over the last few years we also became very good at appointing new managers as a group.

Internal promotion can lead to managers whose average age was going down, but we felt we were successful in promoting people of all ages. Why did we not hire any managers from outside after the start-up phase? It is important to make it clear that we were not opposed to it if we did not find the right talent inside. Getting new "blood" is often an argument made for hiring from the outside. But with a twenty percent staff turnover and constantly appointing new managers, we were in effect getting new "blood" all the time.

One huge benefit of internal promotions was that we were able to run the company in a different way. There is a strong tendency of outside managers to try to implement the structure of their old companies. But the downside of internal promotions can be the loss of input from outside.

As part of a huge company with a healthy exchange of learning from other stores, however, we saw this risk as minimal. There are thousands of books and training classes on how to do it the traditional way.

It is the different way that is often unexplored and harder to do. As long as we constantly kept questioning the way we did things, we felt we kept the organization alive and well.

Compare this example to a garden center or your own garden if you have one. It seems more complicated and more difficult to get a large plant to fit into your garden when compared to growing it from when it is small.

Many times the big one has a hard time adjusting to your soil and your environment.

A gardener takes special care in helping a large (and often expensive) plant make the transition into a new environment. The bigger plant also often has soil with it from its previous garden.

You can see this issue in the corporate world when newly appointed CEOs bring key people with them from their old workplaces. When that does not happen, it is just assumed that the new big plant will fit in. No wonder many new big bosses or coaches in professional sports fail.

HIRING OF RELATIVES

"A large extended family."

Many companies shy away from hiring relatives. They blame security issues and other social problems; however, more than twenty five percent of all staff in our store had a relative working there. It did not happen by design, but what could be a better compliment about our store than someone wanting his or her parent, child, or sibling to work there as well?

There are some small issues that can arise, but if handled with respect they can easily be dealt with. We were delighted to see some of our staff find their mates in the store, relationships that led to marriage several times. With an average employee age around late twenties, this was a natural occurrence. And sometimes one of the staff would have to go on maternity leave. We found reason to celebrate such occasions!

An outside expert did a very thorough study after ten years and found no significant problems with our situation. Here is the summary from the study:

"It is evident that the atmosphere in the store is seen both by its very large group of family members/partners and its nonfamily members as being positively affected by the large percentage of family members working within this organization. The nonfamily members do not seem to have any large concerns over this influence in a negative way. On the contrary, for the most part they agree with it. The results of the survey show that having such a large population of family members/partners working together fosters strong culture within the store and appears to be very beneficial for this organization."

We did have to let go a few husbands, wives, and children, but there were no signs of lingering anger. The way it was done was like this: five minutes before we let the person go, we asked the spouse, parent, or child to come in so we would tell them what was going to happen. No details were given.

We stressed that we were only doing this out of respect for the person who was continuing working for us, so that they would know the situation if the person involved would be upset afterward.

Everyone was of course hired on an individual basis, and we made sure that no close family member could report to another family member. Many of our coworkers commented over the years about the family feeling in the store. Maybe the fact that 25 percent actually had family there contributed to that feeling. In any case, the feeling of family absolutely contributed to the success of our store.

My Own Journey

All these questions about what makes a person grow is quite naturally leading to me! What made me grow? A small-town boy from Sweden thrown out in the big world, first Denmark, Canada, the old East Bloc, and in the end, Seattle. A painful divorce early on in Sweden seemed to set the stage for change. I had to let go of control when I realized there was so little I could control.

Later, meeting a new woman in Canada with a very outgoing personality and endless energy helped bring this shy Swede out of his shell. At the same time, meeting Bjorn (first my boss, later my partner), a person with a fantastic sense of humor and a heart of gold, made me realize the importance of both fun and generosity in business. He gave me endless freedom to do things I had never done before.

Early on in Canada we hired a training person who told me I had a lot of empathy. Not knowing the English language that well, I had to look it up what the word meant. I felt really good about that comment! It made me grow.

At first I was the controller in Canada for eight stores, and later I became the sales and marketing responsible for both the United States and Canada. The Canadian side of our organization was responsible for opening the first two stores in the United States. However, when I was appointed company president in Canada, I still felt very inept as a leader. I did two things: first I read any leadership book I could get my hands on (Warren Bennis's On Becoming a Leader quickly became my favorite). Second I started to work with a Swedish consultant, who had a profound impact on my development. Before saying yes to working with me, she insisted on spending a weekend with me and my family in order to determine if I was serious about personal growth. This led to fifteen years of very rewarding cooperation.

What did I then have to face? Many of the things you have already read about in this book, like dealing with my niceness and my need to be liked. I was overly nice for a long time, and then I would suddenly blow up in anger. I was really fumbling over how to be soft and strong at the same time.

I can't point to a single event that created a major change; there were just many small almost invisible changes. It's a process that is still ongoing. Like how to become better at letting go, whether it's a habit, belief in a scenario, or a person who I want to see a change in but he or she is either not ready or doesn't want it. During my time working in the old East Bloc, my position was such that I dealt with the founder of the parent company a lot. I realized quickly that my skin was not thick enough for that environment. Every summer I had to spend a week with a psychologist (who also had a profound impact on me) in his training seminars to scream out my frustration over my inability to cope with playing with the big "dogs".

By working in a much more political climate with very limited openness, I formed my opinions of what I wanted to have if I got the chance. I also became less and less dependent on being liked and found that it was much more important to be respected in the long run. To show vulnerability became easier. I had to stay true to who I was.

I certainly did not see myself as a great leader, although I did have a strong tenacity to develop myself. My partner once called me a seeker. Yes, I am driven to learn more about why I react and what upsets me and what makes me tick. If that is a seeker—that's me. When we were given a chance to open our own store, my partner and I sat down and wrote about the things we felt were most important. As long-term friends we often saw things in very much the same way. What was most important was to have one team, one store, not many teams in the same store. We really wanted to give our staff similar freedom with responsibility that we had been given in this company. I also had an intense passion to help people grow.

Did we make many mistakes? Oh so many that it would take another book to list them all.

I was once invited to sit on a prestigious panel of business leaders. We were asked the question: "What keeps you awake at night?" I deliberately went last since I knew my answer would be weird. After listening to the rest of the panel voice concerns about rising interest rates or other macroeconomics, I said, "What keeps me awake is my shortcomings in handling my staff." Our focus was to take care of staff members who would then take care of our customers.

At one time I was so frustrated about our shortcomings in hiring the right staff that I started to keep a scorecard in my day planner of things like first impression, handshake, etc. We tended to hire more outgoing personalities since we were in retail, but many of them did not last long. They seemed to get bored.

One time I looked for a meek personality, just to try something different. She is still with the big company and has a great career. There is nothing meek about her now. At the time she was hired, she had problems at home (which I did not know), and that might have made her appear weaker.

The humbling part is that people change and their lives change. I never saw myself as having the career I had. It just evolved step by step. I believe that a lot in life is about doing it!

I was once very frustrated that we just sat around talking and talking and not taking action. One of my store managers at the time came up with a 3D model. "Discuss, Decide, Do it!" The size of the letters symbolized how we saw the importance of the three activities.

Another manager, who I had many reasons to try to coach, always said after our meetings: "Thank you so much for pointing out my shortcomings!" I felt so miserable for two reasons. First he had only heard the shortcomings and not the good things I had said about him. Second I really don't believe in working on your shortcomings!

I really believe in focusing on what you are good at. Sure, from time to time we get some good insight from other people about things we could do better, but we grow more if someone tells us what we are doing well.

Most of us are painfully aware of our shortcomings, but we don't seem to see the things we can do and what we do well. In the end the shortcoming manager and I had to part ways. He had to leave our store.

Sometimes there is only so much you can do to help. We had decided early to err on the side of patience, giving our staff numerous chances before asking them to leave or step down.

When I look at the mistakes I have made, they mostly center on not seeing ineffective situations earlier. I really wanted success, both for myself and for others, and therefore I did not always act fast enough. What's confusing is that we were amply rewarded in some cases when we had been overly patient.

Many people I have worked with who now have incredible careers within the company were close to being let go at some point in their careers.

We stuck by them, and they were able to focus on their strengths and let go of their shortcomings.

In the early years of my life I was led to believe that I could learn and do many things. Interestingly enough, none of them was in the area of sports. So now that I am retired and have lots of time to learn to play tennis and golf, I am painfully aware of how important it is to believe you can do it. Taking lessons often means that someone points out my shortcomings. It seldom involves getting feedback on how good I am. I believe this translates so easily to our work. There I had enough people giving me encouragement and telling me I could do things.

Early on I was far too eager to please and showed anger too easily. I don't agree at all with people who say, "Don't let them see you sweat." I had trouble showing enough of my softer side; I just showed the angry side, which threw me off balance. But as the years went by, I learned to become more direct without being emotionally attached and at the same time not being afraid of shedding a tear or showing a softer feeling.

END RESULT

"It seemed like the steps we laid out for everyone over how to succeed caught fire. It was normal to try to grow and learn."

As we said in the beginning, we wanted to help grow both our business and our coworkers while having fun! Our bottom line remained healthy through all those years. We did pay our coworkers more than other stores on the US side of the company, which seemed to lead to higher caliber coworkers who were almost never absent and who worked really hard for us.

It seemed the more we invested in our coworkers, the more we got back. When we started out, my partner and I had very low expectations on the financial rewards of our venture. We expected to receive fair pay for our work and to be able to work not only for ourselves but also for the company we loved.

We were just happy to be able to try different things.

In the end the results exceeded our wildest dreams! Our goal was to grow our company and coworkers while having fun. Did we grow the company? Yes, from $25 million in sales to $142 million, with the number of staff growing from 125 to nearly 600.

Did we grow our coworkers? We sent out more than sixty fantastic coworkers to other corporate units around the world, many of them having great careers even if they are only at the beginning of them. One of our most satisfying moments was to see one of our coworkers succeed within the parent company. To see someone start with us as a part-timer, then full-timer, then area responsible, then leader for a small department, then a bigger department, then running the whole store, then responsible for several stores or warehouses in the big company and then...(The story is still unfolding.).

This was more than we could have dreamed of! We really felt we had succeeded as gardeners. We have numerous examples of this kind of development, so it was not just a one-hit wonder. For us this was the final proof that what we did really worked!

We also got a side benefit we'd never counted on. At our farewell party we heard from many of the families of our coworkers that we had not only grown coworkers but they had in turn inspired their families to grow! The garden center had inspired growth well outside the actual greenhouse!

Yes, we were lucky, with good timing, good staff, good relations with the city, and great customers. But we were also relentless gardeners who never gave up and who always believed we could keep growing both as individuals and as a company.

It is interesting that since we never got anyone to help us build a regular store, we ended up in a series of warehouses in which we were able to take on more and more space as we kept growing. As our neighbor Boeing scaled down its operations, we kept growing ours. So while our plants were growing, our greenhouses could also be enlarged.

Now It's Up to You!

Okay, now you have read the book and you might (hopefully) like it or parts thereof. You may want to make some changes to your organization. How should you approach it?

Thirteen steps to successful change:

1. Go to a mirror and take a look at the person you see there—that's where you start. Do you have the courage to look at yourself and make your own changes? What do you need to let go off? Do you have a passion for supporting others in their growth, or is this just about fixing a problem in your organization?

2. Think long-term. This is not a recipe for a quick fix. Be prepared to be in it for the long haul.

3. Be ready to take chances on people. Since not everyone will grow, you need to work with as many as possible. Plants grow at their own pace. You have to give yourself choices.

4. Give your people more freedom than you can bear. It should give you some worries at least. No one is 100 percent ready when they take on a new job.

5. Confront with love and confront often! With increased freedom comes huge responsibility. You still have goals to meet. Niceness does not cut it! Neither do fear tactics.

6. Pay close attention to the how, not only the what. See how your people deal with difficult tasks.

7. Remember, the only thing you want is success, for your people and in the end for yourself. To throw people out in deep water without some help in the form of support or a lifeline is irresponsible. You need to provide both trust and support.

8. Just because other companies are doing something, does not mean it's the best way. Have the courage to be different, but keep it simple.

9. Examine leadership at all levels. I used to say, "Leadership has to start long before you are appointed manager. Leadership needs to be nurtured and encouraged at all levels."

10. One of the most effective ways to kill good leadership and business development is to have lots of rules, especially rules that people have to follow to keep their jobs. So look over the rule book to see what can be eliminated other than safety rules and rules of conduct. Your organization must be built on trust to succeed in growing your plants. I have never worked for someone I did not trust, meaning that I felt they were competent and that they cared about me. Encourage your people to do the same. I feel that many companies have a huge fear of their staff making mistakes. It is often used as an excuse for more rules and more control. It leads to no one daring to do anything extra, no innovation, and no risk taking.

11. Remember, to be good at anything, you have to practice. Encourage sharing difficulty in leadership among the leaders, yourself included! Don't feel silly to role-play. See it as a practice court. A good gardener is always looking for a better way.

12. Of all the things we did, I like the idea of personal plan of action the best. Insist on it! Talk is cheap. Only do it counts.

13. Don't be surprised that after you have done all this, someone's partner or spouse will thank you for changing their lives. There is no separation between a healthy work life and a healthy home life. Good things will happen in both places.

Good luck!

"The only way to put good leadership into practice ... is to practice."

APPENDIX

The following are the fundamentals from our training programs. The training ideas have been developed through my own personal work done over many years with different consultants. Most of the experiential learning that follows was supervised by licensed professionals.

The Foundation for Our Leadership Training

- The only way to put good leadership in practice is to...practice!
- Our work is based on the premise that "we cannot learn you anything," meaning that each of us has to do our own learning.
- Learning and change happen only in the present.
- No serious work can be done without honesty and openness.

We believe that to make any training in the areas of personal development and leadership effective, it has to "touch" you. We need to be able to not only talk to your brain, but also to "touch" your heart. There has to be a feeling connected to the experience. It might be joy or it could be sadness. To take on a new skill often means you must let go of an ineffective one.

We truly believe in experiential learning. That means active participation, with often your whole body involved. It means that participants are put on the spot, or out of their comfort zones as one of our participants used to say. It does not mean talking about your past. Our focus was always on the here and now.

What and How

Why is *how* you do things so important? Just look at how you can say the words "I love you." You can say them with passion, or you can say them without emotion and underlying meaning. Many businesses concentrate on explaining *what* should be done and leave the *how* up to the individual to figure out. We believe how you do things is 80 percent of success in communication.

Obstacles in Becoming a More Effective Supervisor/Leader

1. Little or no awareness about how your personal issues impact your effectiveness at work
2. Seeking too little or too much help (dependency)
3. Lack of trust in self and others
4. Lack of courage to make necessary changes

Change

Change is one of the hardest things to embrace and accomplish. A lot of people crave change, but it is often change of the physical environment only. For example: you are unhappy with your boss at one place of employment. Many people change jobs and then find a new boss to be unhappy with. Compare this with people who try to find the right partner. Some people are unhappy with whomever they have for a partner at the time.

It is in such situations that it is time to look at ourselves and see if we need to change first. To go from the present situation to a changed situation, we need to cross a place we call the "ocean of nothingness," a place where we have nothing to hold on to. It is neither the old place nor the new wished-for place. Most of us want to hold on to the old while changing, which makes true change impossible. Compare to holding on to an old boyfriend or girlfriend while starting to see a new one. This is not a recipe for success. The letting go part is the most difficult of any change process. For this process to happen, we need a lot of courage. The only thing others can do for us is to give us en-courage-ment.

Here is an illustrated example of how we view it:

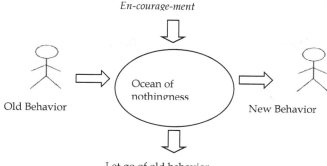

William Bridges describes transition and change: "The transition process ends the old and begins the new.

Between ending and beginning is the emptiness of the neutral zone, the chaos from which all new life flows. Without the neutral zone, there would be no rebirth. I know that we avoid endings whenever possible and steer clear whenever we can of neutral-zone emptiness. Endings feel like failures to us, but at a deeper level they awaken in us the fear of death."

One other aspect of change is that it sometimes happens unexpectedly through force, like losing a job, a serious illness, a sudden romantic breakup, or the death or illness of someone close to us. All this will help prompt the change process, although there are no guarantees. There are people who have had three heart attacks and still haven't seriously changed their lifestyles.

We never asked people to make dramatic changes. Instead we used the word tweak in reference to changing their behaviors. (Remember the dial on old-time radios.) If you are a little off from the station, it sounds awful, but when you are right there, wonderful music can come out of your radio. Most of us only need to tweak our behaviors, yet this concept still appears so frightening to most of us.

We also encouraged our leaders to use their best resource, meaning their staff, to find out how effective their staff was. In an honest, open environment, you can actually learn a lot from a simple, nonthreatening conversation. Most companies like to use fancy and expensive questionnaires to determine how their employees are doing. In a hostile work environment, that might be the only way.

Here are some sayings we used:

- If you do what you always did, you always get what you always got.
- As in skiing, if you never fall, you probably never improve your skills.
- Dare to stay in the questions without hastily jumping to the answers.
- Do not hold others responsible for your feelings, actions, and circumstances.
- What you resist persists. Until you really face the necessary change, the problem will not go away.
- When we stop changing, we are pronounced dead.

Trace Problems

We often concern ourselves with what we call trace problems.

Examples:

If only my boss would be _____, then I would be_____.

If only my wife would not_____, then I would be _____.

If only my shoulder would not hurt, then I could _____.

If only my parents would have ____, then I could have _____.

It is important to look at what is underneath the actual problem. We tend to hold on to these trace problems and avoid dealing with what is underneath, since that might necessitate a real change. It is often a good excuse not to take charge of your life.

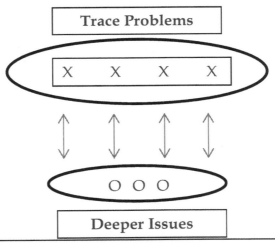

Leadership Walk

One of the most effective exercises for discovering learning opportunities with regard to leadership was what we called the Leadership Walk, a somewhat nerve-wracking exercise if taken too seriously, but it was a very effective one.

The participants (generally not less than ten and not more than twenty individuals) stood in a circle with lots of space inside. One person was asked to be the coworker and start walking in the circle in pattern, with no pattern also considered a pattern. The coworker was also asked to be himself or herself, so if he or she felt that he or she was a tricky employee, he or she should also be in that circle. Then the rest of the participants were asked if they wanted to be the supervisor. They were encouraged to try to feel if this particular coworker would be difficult for them to lead. The harder it felt, the more we encouraged them to jump in to be the supervisor.

Their job was to change the pattern without using any words or sound whatsoever, and of course only touching that was appropriate to the coworker was allowed. Sometimes touch was not accepted by the "walker" at all.

We also encouraged the supervisor to use a minimum of nonverbal actions to adjust the behavior of the coworker. Less is more. Even though it was uncomfortable to be put on the spot like this, the learning was immense.

Too soft, too hard, too little respect, etc...all came out in this exercise if taken seriously. We adjusted; we got feedback from not only the coworker, but from the other participants in order to help the supervisor be effective. In the end we wanted to see successful leadership.

Our Ideas with Regard to Communication

- Comm-uni-cation means coming together—oneness

- Two levels of communication
  1) Content—WHAT—20 percent of the job is application; surface problems slow down content application.
  2) Process—HOW—80 percent is how we say something

- How is the stance of the person: open/closed? What do you read from their body? Verbal is the slowest part of communication. We send out signals without words using our body language. Ex: I love you—arms folded, etc.

- Learn to sense the movement; what's the feeling coming through?

- The feeling connects with the process—where is the person now?

- What is the underlying reason for the communication? Is there a need, or is it for contact only?

- At the point of communication, there are two things going on:
  1) Intrapersonal—what's going on inside me?
  2) Interpersonal—what's going on between us?

• We cannot eliminate that something is going on inside of ourselves, but if we are aware of it, we can minimize its effect on our communication. You might have had a fight with your spouse this morning, but how effective will you be in your contact at work if you hang on to that situation?

Boundaries

We are looking for balance in how we communicate. What kinds of boundaries do we have? This was especially important for us when we were dealing with fifty thousand visitors to our store per week! Some of our customers might already have had an unrelated problem that they brought with them, which might have aggravated a situation.

• A boundary is the border that sets the system apart from the environment. Human systems have physical boundaries (skin), and psychological boundaries (attitudes, values, beliefs).

- The quality of our communication depends on how open or closed our psychological boundaries are.
- When boundaries are open—we take in too much—we absorb too much—we have trouble figuring out the meaning of different messages, which leads to confusion and overloading from our processing capacities.
- When boundaries are closed—we take in too little and we are overly concerned with the meaning of different messages, which leads to a lack of awareness.
- Boundaries need to be firm and flexible/permeable, so that the needed information comes in. We need to be able to adjust our boundaries for different situations.
- Closed—stops at the surface/open/absorb takes it in to core. Example: a customer yells at us; we can either take it in and we can choose to let it affect us for the day, or we can choose to have a firmer boundary and stay neutral and deal with the issue in a more compassionate way.

- The goal is to be open and have protection at the same time. Can I have both firm and flexible boundaries? Be aware of what we take in or not. For example: Are you picking up chewing gum off the street.

Picture Drawing

In one-on-one sessions we sometimes asked our coworkers to draw a picture of how they saw themselves within our organization. They were to use feelings about how their relationship was with the organization and the department they worked in, rather than giving us an organizational chart. We asked them to make sure they were in the picture and to use different colors for different flows; that is, task and information versus support and care. We asked them to draw those flows and gave them only a few minutes to ensure it was more of a gut feeling than a lot of thinking involved.

After the picture was done we looked at it together. Our job was to ask questions to help the coworker understand the picture better.

For example, one good leader had a tough time making up her mind over what she wanted to do with her life, both personally and professionally within the company. If I had used traditional methods, I might have had trouble coaching her. She might have become defensive about it. But when she showed me her picture, she had drawn herself sitting on a fence! Then my only job was to see how I could support her in actually making and following through on her decisions.

Another good leader drew herself as just a head. When I asked her what would happen if she brought the whole body into the company, she said she would be concerned over not being a good mother. This lead to her having a great evening conversation with her children about this, and she was relieved that she could actually see a way in which she could continue to be a good mother and also bring all of her skills to our store. It appears that we seem to imagine problems that, when more carefully looked at, may not be real.

In summary

This has been a very brief overview over our training. It would take a book by itself to fully go through all our exercises. I just included the most important ones. With help of also other literature and your imagination, I hope you can come up with the training that fits your purposes. What is important is that the training you provide gives the participants the chance to have an experiential learning. The training has to " touch" us on more than on an information level. The learning has to be put into practice by practicing so we can gain confidence and truly believe we can do it ourselves. I will end by repeating my favorite quote, which can also be applicable on training and trainers.

"When the best leader's work is done, the people say, 'We did it ourselves!'"—Lao Tzu